ANGLESEY FROM THE SEA

ANGLESEY FROM THE SEA

An armchair journey

by

MARGARET HUGHES

ISBN: 0-86381-698-3

First published in 2001 by
Gwasg Carreg Gwalch, 12 Iard yr Orsaf, Llanrwst, Wales LL26 0EH
☎ 01492 642031   🖷 01492 641502
✆ books@carreg-gwalch.co.uk   Internet: www.carreg-gwalch.co.uk

For John and Mair Heywood Thomas
for whom Anglesey is 'Fron Heulog'.

The author wishes to acknowledge generous co-operation from
Alison Lea-Wilson of the Anglesey Sea Zoo, the Countryside
Commission for Wales, Bangor; Trinity House, Swansea; and
Magnox Electric PLC at Wylfa. Also Handel Evans at Llangefni
Public Library and the staff at Menai Bridge Library, and to
Geraint Davies, J.C. Davies and Ed. Pari-Jones for photographic
illustrations.

And to Myrddin ap Dafydd and the staff at Gwasg Carreg
Gwalch for their ever-pleasant professional co-operation.

Contents

ANGLESEY – *YNYS MÔN*

The island's history is one of a series of invasions and various marauders have called it by different names. The Vikings called it *Anglesey* – 'island in the strait' but the Romans paid homage to the Celtic inhabitants they found here, calling it by its Brythonic name, *Mona*. In the Welsh language, which evolved from the Brythonic tongue in the 6th century, it is called 'Ynys Môn' (*ynys* meaning island) and today this term is used more widely than ever before.

Introduction

Fireside map-reading can be as addictive as browsing through a seed catalogue when the weather and the season preclude any outside activity.

The map-reader, with very little expertise, can recall places and experiences enjoyed in the past. Or, if the area is new territory, the simple ordnance survey symbols are as effective as words and pictures. Add to these some background historical and topographical knowledge, then hours spent with a map and an informative guide can whisk one away from dark days and plummeting temperatures. There are vistas to view, characters to meet, stories to read. The armchair sailor around Anglesey *(Ynys Môn)* needs neither chart nor tide table.

Before the two bridges linking the island with mainland Wales were built, Anglesey *(Ynys Môn)* was relatively isolated and development was slow.

Until Thomas Telford completed his suspension bridge in 1828, and the tortuous approach road along the coast from Conwy was by-passed by his new London-Holyhead road through the mountains, access was by ferry. It was hazardous. It is small wonder that the inhabitants looked west to Dublin for their business and social activities, and the port of Holyhead *(Caergybi)* became the main access and departure point.

Telford's new road brought instant relief. The approach to the island was eased further when the railway was carried over the water by Stephenson's Britannia tubular bridge in 1850.

It was not until after the Second World War, however, that Anglesey *(Ynys Môn)* began to enjoy modern amenities in every corner of the island – piped water, improved roads, a more widely available electricity supply – all bringing in their wake an increase in tourism which brought the island to the notice of a wider public, and boosted the local economy.

The atomic energy plant at Wylfa in the north prompted great improvements in the road system. Today this has changed again, with the dualling of Telford's road across to Holyhead *(Caergybi)*. But there are still corners of the island which remain secret, many of them to be seen at best from the sea. So the sailor has the advantage of a fresh outlook.

Many visitors have their first impression of Anglesey *(Ynys Môn)* as they approach across the narrowest part of the Menai Strait at Menai Bridge *(Porthaethwy)*. So, with an appropriate ordnance survey map at hand, let us take a look at the little town from the Strait, and be ready to set sail in a south-westerly direction under Telford's suspension bridge.

Menai Bridge *(Porthaethwy)*

To appreciate the complications of sailing through the Menai Strait *(Afon Menai)*, one must understand its unusual tidal pattern.

The eighteen miles (29km) long Strait has two high tides and two low tides each day. On the flood tide, from low to high water, sea water enters the Strait through the narrow funnel between Anglesey *(Ynys Môn)* and Caernarfon at Abermenai, its south-western end. At the same time, water flows around Anglesey *(Ynys Môn)* and enters the north-eastern end of the Strait at Puffin Island *(Ynys Seiriol)*. These two tides meet between the two bridges when, for a while, there is no horizontal flow but the water level continues to rise. At the point when the north-easterly stream overcomes that from the south-west, all the water begins to flow back towards the south-west. The tide ebbs (from high to low water) and as low water approaches the last of the tide in the north-east changes direction and flows back past Beaumaris to the open sea.

Tidal currents between the bridges can be swift, reaching eight knots. The floor of the Strait here is rocky, but relatively shallow except for one or two deep pools, and the Anglesey *(Ynys Môn)* shore is dotted with small islands. The sailor passing through the Strait at its narrowest point is guided by the warning beacon on the Swellies Rock, marking Pwll Ceris which can be especially dangerous to the uninitiated.

Long before the bridges across the Menai Strait were built, Menai Bridge *(Porthaethwy)* was the crossing point for cattle.

What is now the Cambria Inn was, in 1688, the Menai Bridge *(Porthaethwy)* ferry house. The old Horse Ferry, as it was called, had been in existence since the 13th century. Originally it belonged to the Crown but, when superseded by the suspension bridge the then owner, Miss Silence Williams, was paid £26,934 in compensation for loss of dues which then amounted to around £900 per annum.

A contemporary writer commented, 'to watch cattle loudly protesting at being forced to swim the Strait from Ynys y Moch was a sight not easily forgotten, with the beasts terrified of the waves and the strong currents, and the drovers behaving as if they were themselves hardly better than beasts'.

For many years Menai Bridge *(Porthaethwy)* was the venue of an important cattle fair. Since 1691 this had been held near the Antelope Inn on the mainland shore, but early in the 1800s it was transferred to Menai Bridge *(Porthaethwy)* as Anglesey *(Ynys Môn)* farmers objected to risking the lives of their cattle during the hazardous crossing. The cattle fair was accompanied by the usual trappings of side shows and stalls to tempt those who made the occasion a holiday – probably their only holiday in the year – and the streets would be thronged with country people out to enjoy themselves. The cattle fair is no longer. But the fun fair and stalls remain as Menai Bridge *(Porthaethwy)* remembers its past and celebrates 'Ffair Borth' each October.

There had been talk of bridging the Strait since the 1770s when a Mr Golborne submitted a plan for an embankment out from both shores with a bridge at the centre. In 1785 a timber construction was suggested with a swivel or drawbridge in the middle, this to cross from the Bangor shore to Ynys Gaint. In 1802 and 1811 Rennie and Telford both submitted plans for a stone and iron construction.

All these were rejected as they obstructed navigation. The final, accepted design was presented by Thomas Telford in 1818, for a suspension bridge rising 100 feet (30m) above high water level to allow tall ships to sail beneath. The western pier would stand on Ynys y Moch, a rock so called because this was where pigs would break their dangerous swim to the mainland as they were driven to the English markets.

Work on the bridge began in 1819. All sea traffic was stopped, and blasting began on Ynys y Moch. Stone came from the quarries at Penmon, carried to the Bangor ferry by coasters. Lord Warren Bulkeley who owned the quarry was paid 6d per ton by the government.

In his autobiography Telford writes: 'During the erection of the bridge many of the more industrious workmen employed their leisure hours by polishing waste pieces of this beautiful and frequently variegated marble, and forming them into letter pressers, ink stands and chimney ornaments neatly executed, which have been eagerly bought by visitors who come to see progress.'

It was not until April 15, 1822, that building was far enough advanced for the first chain to be thrown across the Strait. There were great celebrations. Flags flew, pleasure boats plied up and down the water within safe distance, and crowds gathered.

A raft 450 feet (137m) and six feet (1.8m) wide was moved into position, supporting the part of the chain to be drawn over. Towed by four boats, it was assisted by the tide to draw it into position midstream and then it was tied up to several buoys. Another part of the chain hung from the top of the pier on the Bangor side, almost down to high water. The end of the chain on the raft was fastened to two blocks so that it could be hoisted to the top of the pier on the Anglesey *(Ynys Môn)* side.

Four fifers, playing lively tunes, kept one hundred and twenty-eight men working in rhythm as they manned four capstans. The whole process was completed without a hitch and took two hours and twenty minutes. Telford himself was on hand to join the two wrought iron chains together.

Then came an unexpected climax. Three of the workmen, a stone mason, a labourer and a carpenter, crept slowly and precariously, Blondin-fashion, from one side to the other along the newly joined chain, while a band played and the crowd held its breath.

The financial cost of the Menai Suspension Bridge *(Pont y Borth)* was £120,000, but four men lost their lives during its erection.

Tolls were charged for crossing until the late 1930s. An increase in the type and weight of traffic over the years has called for adaptation. The original wrought iron chains have been replaced by steel. A weight restriction of seven and a half tons was introduced in 1989 and the carriageway was strengthened. The walk-ways have been carried around the outside of the piers to allow more room for vehicles. At the end of 1999 the bridge was closed to traffic for three months to allow a new and stronger road to be built. Maintenance, in the form of strength checks and painting, is continuous.

The suspension bridge brought economic changes to Menai Bridge *(Porthaethwy)*. The population of the town increased and the area appeared set fair to do business. Richard Davies, a local merchant with entrepreneurial flair saw the opportunity to sell goods bought cheaply in Liverpool at points on the Anglesey *(Ynys Môn)*, coast where they could be off-loaded from the ship into warehouses and Menai Bridge *(Porthaethwy)* was one of these venues.

In 1828 Richard Davies leased from the Marquess of Anglesey a plot of land near the shore where he opened a timber yard. He took shares in small vessels which brought flour, sugar, hardware, timber and iron to Menai Bridge *(Porthaethwy)*. Eventually he bought his own ship, and in 1843 began to transport slate and emigrants to America from the Menai Strait, bringing back timber. It was said at the time that his emigrants crossed the Atlantic under better conditions than those sailing from Liverpool. By 1846 the Davies family had three more ships.

During the 1870s the Menai Strait was a busy seaway with over seven hundred ships registered at its several small ports.

Large houses on the Bangor side of the Strait belonged to the Davies family. 'Ceris', the red brick house below the mainland entrance to the bridge, is now a nursing home. 'Bodlondeb', the gracious grey building opposite the pier has been converted into apartments, and 'Treborth', hidden in woods on the Caernarfonshire side between the two bridges, is now a school.

The Davies family built the English Presbyterian church in Menai Bridge *(Porthaethwy)* whose spire can be glimpsed from the water. They are remembered by a memorial inside the handsome building. The class-conscious Victorian family entered by their own private door, to worship in the family pew.

Tourism became a major industry in Wales following the provision of easier access, and Menai Bridge *(Porthaethwy)* benefitted through regular and frequent sailings by pleasure steamers calling at the pier. *St Tudno, La Marguerite,* and *St Seiriol* were familiar sights as they brought holiday-makers from Liverpool and Llandudno.

The view of Menai Bridge *(Porthaethwy)* from the water is now dominated by the modern, functional buildings of the School of Ocean Sciences of the University of Wales, Bangor. This is the largest university centre teaching marine sciences in Britain, and one of the largest in Europe.

The school is situated within a few metres of the sea, enabling students to collect data at sea, in the estuaries and on the sea-shore. Bass, cod, whiting, conger eels and plaice are found in the Menai Strait, as well as rare sea anemones and sponges.

The school has operated its own custom-built, ocean-going research ship, 'Prince Madog', the only large vessel of this type operated by a UK university and moored, in between sailings, at St George's Pier below the department buildings. The ship has now made her final voyage and is due to be replaced by a more up-to-date vessel.

During the summer months regattas and races attract sailing clubs from Caernarfon to Conwy, as well as members of the Royal Anglesey Yacht Club, the Royal Welsh and the Royal Dee Yacht Clubs.

Menai Suspension Bridge *(Pont y Borth)* to Britannia Bridge *(Pont Britannia)*

Sailing between the great piers of the Menai Suspension Bridge *(Pont y Borth)* is the best way of appreciating the immensity of Telford's masterpiece.

A lane follows the Anglesey *(Ynys Môn)* shoreline, past a stone-built house called 'Summercourt' which Thomas Telford used as a base while his bridge was under construction. This lane leads to an attractive walker's way known locally as the Belgian Promenade, and to a causeway over which worshippers and sightseers pass on to Ynys Llantysilio *(Church Island)*. The promenade was built during the First World War to give employment to Flemish refugees. After restoration in 1965 it was re-opened by one of the men who had helped to build it, M. Edouard Willems of Bonheide. The woods clothing the hill, 'Coed Cyrnol', were named after Colonel Sandys who lived nearby at the turn of the 19th century.

Of the several islands dotted in the Strait, Ynys Llantysilio *(Church Island)* is the largest. The tiny church of Sant Tysilio probably dates back to the 15th century, but stands on the site of an earlier foundation, as suggested by the date 630 AD above the door. Island sites such as this were favoured by the early saints, as they offered seclusion for a contemplative life of prayer and meditation. Our armchair journey around the Anglesey *(Ynys Môn)* coast will reveal several more. The tiny church of Sant Tysilio has a pervading atmosphere of tranquillity.

The views from the island are spectacular, especially to the west where Britannia Bridge *(Pont Britannia)* spans the water. Closer to hand the green fields of Anglesey *(Ynys Môn)* fall gently down to the shore, the haunt of many sea birds. Two smaller islands, Ynys Welltog and Ynys Benlas, are in fact the tops of a rocky ridge below the surface, even at low water. There is a wide variety of marine life between the two bridges, and botanists find much to interest them around the fringes of the Strait's small islands.

The light marking Pwll Ceris was added to an existing marker some years ago, its fixing creating a stir as it was delivered by helicopter.

During the 1940s and in to the '50s one of the sights which attracted the attention of visitors was the one-time man-of-war, the 92-gun battleship *Nile*, converted to a school ship and re-named *Conway*. She was due to be re-fitted in Liverpool in April 1953 and began the difficult manoeuvre from her anchorage off the Caernarfon shore with the help of two tugs. Due to what is now considered to have been faulty navigation, and probably ignorance or misunderstanding of the very exact timing required to take advantage of the tide to be able to sail safely past the Swellies, the ship fouled on the nearby rocks known as the Platters, where she broke her back.

Elderly residents still recall the event and its sad conclusion. Three years later, when ship-breakers moved in with oxy-acetylene equipment to dispose of the wreck, the old wooden hulk caught fire, and all that remained of her sank out of sight.

Land along the shore, known appropriately as 'Cae Glan Môr' was given to the Natural Trust by two families in 1938 and 1980, to perpetuate the incomparable view from the road. A lay-by was provided where visitors can stop to appreciate the view across to the mountains and both bridges. This must surely be the most photographed view in North Wales.

Ynys Gorad Goch *(the island of the red weir)*, with its white-painted buildings, lies just below the Britannia Bridge *(Pont Britannia)*. It has a long and interesting history. At low water, two weirs are evident, to the north and south, which give the clue to the island's story.

There are several fisheries hereabouts. The earliest known document relating to Ynys Gorad Goch is dated 1590 when it belonged to the Bangor Diocese and was leased to Thomas Fletcher of Treborth for 'three pounds and besides one barell

14

full of hearinges at the tyme of the hearinge fishinge'. An early map refers to it as 'Bishop's Island'. There is a room in the house with a central window, over which is a carving of a mitre and an inscription 'I.R.1808', referring to Bishop Randolph of Bangor who, it was claimed, came here to meditate.

Since 1888, when the Ecclesiastical Commissioners sold the island, it has been in private hands, and is now part of an outward-bound project.

Fishing by stopping the mouths of tidal creeks with brushwood and stones was possibly one of the earliest methods used by man. At Ynys Gorad Goch the tides were used in the same way, and the angles of the weirs were set to catch the maximum quantities of fish passing through the Strait on the ebb tide. The separate building with a tower was a curing house. The fish traps caught bream, codling, dogfish, herring, garfish, gurnard, mackerel, plaice, pollack, salmon, sand eels, whitebait and whiting.

During private occupation earlier in the 20th century the residents did a popular summer trade by providing whitebait teas to visitors who would walk down to the shore through the Coed Môr woods, ring a bell to summon a rowing boat to carry them over to the island and enjoy a pot of tea, brown bread and butter and fried whitebait in a basket, all for one shilling.

Britannia Bridge *(Pont Britannia)* today appears very different from the original design which consisted of parallel iron tubes through which the railway ran, and were a prototype for box girder construction.

Coach travel had been superseded by the new steam trains by the middle of the 19th century, and there was an outcry for a bridge to be built across the Strait to carry the railway on to Holyhead *(Caergybi)* the port for Ireland. It was from here, on what is now a tree-clad shore, that Robert Stephenson supervised the building of his great tubular bridge.

Along the Caernarfon shore a platform half a mile (800m) long, covering three and a half acres, was constructed out into the water, on which seven hundred men worked piecing together the huge metal plates to form the tubes. There were three large workshops for forges and the various machinery for punching and cutting plate iron.

Five wharves coped with ships bringing iron from Liverpool, marble from Penmon, and red sandstone from Runcorn. Another eight hundred men worked on the massive stone piers, first making a core of sandstone then lining it with Anglesey *(Ynys Môn)* marble.

To accommodate these workers, many of whom had come from Yorkshire and Cheshire, temporary shanties and small wooden cottages sprang up nearby. There was a school for the children of the workers. Sanitary conditions were primitive and it could not have been a pleasant place to live.

Much of the iron work could be done only when the weather was fair, so night work was common. The iron plates, which formed the tubes, had to be riveted together and this was done when there was no wind. The resident engineer kept an account of progress and he described the sight across the water as darkness fell as 'fantastic and unforgettable'. Forty-eight rivet hearths pricked the Caernarfon shore with flickering points of flame, and golden sprays of sparks shot upwards as rivet-boys hurled the white hot bolts forty feet into the air to their counterparts on top of the tubes.

But the event that excited even more curiosity and wonder was when the tubes were floated into mid-stream and hoisted to the top of the piers. It happened on a fine June day, and engineer Brunel accompanied Stephenson to see it. Crowds gathered and booths along the shore housed sideshows and fortune-tellers. There was a holiday atmosphere while everyone watched, fascinated, as the huge tubes were manoeuvred carefully into position below the piers by capstans on both banks. Then came the breath-taking sight of the tubes rising, inch by inch, minute by minute, until they rested safely in their permanent home. Britannia Bridge *(Pont Britannia)* was completed and opened to traffic in 1850.

The platform, the shanties and the crowds are now part of history. But a stone memorial column in Llanfair Pwllgwyngyll churchyard, whose tip can be seen over the trees, reminds us that the Britannia Bridge *(Pont Britannia)* took its toll. The column was erected in memory of the eighteen who died during construction. William Brook of Dewsbury, twenty-seven years of age, was principal accountant of the masonry contractor. He died of typhus fever in 1847, a victim of the living conditions. Emma Greave, the five-years-old daughter of James Greave of Wakefield 'died at Britannia Bridge'. We are not told how or why, but there were so many dangers that could have caused her death.

The story of the Britannia Bridge *(Pont Britannia)* does not end there. One night in 1970 the old bridge was destroyed by fire, begun when boys bent on mischief lit newspapers and threw them into the tubes to disturb bats. They lodged in the roof which was wooden with a bituminous covering, and the blaze became so fierce that the tubes buckled.

This happened at a time when increased road traffic through Menai Bridge *(Porthaethwy)* and Bangor was creating problems, so it was decided to rebuild the bridge with a double deck, allowing for rail traffic below and a new road to link with the A55 above. The new bridge was opened by the Prince of Wales in 1976.

But this, too, took its human toll, as the added names on the memorial column remind us.

One feature of the first bridge remains. Four stone lions, two at each end, guard the rail track. They were sculpted in 1848 by John Thomas, a Gloucestershire sculptor who was also responsible for the stone statues on the north and south fronts of the House of Commons the panels of which bear the arms of the kings and queens of England, the statues and bosses for the Victoria Tower, and the bosses in Saint Stephen's Hall.

The stone lions are twenty-five feet (7.6m) long and weigh eighty tons each.

Britannia Bridge *(Pont Britannia)*
to Plas Newydd

Dominating the skyline above Britannia Bridge *(Pont Britannia)* is the Anglesey Column, towering 91 feet (28m) above Craig y Ddinas, the site of an ancient Early Welsh fortress. The prominent memorial was erected in 1817, two years after the Battle of Waterloo, in honour of Henry William Paget, Earl of Uxbridge whose home, Plas Newydd, can be seen from its high platform. Uxbridge was second in command to Wellington. In the battle he lost his right leg by almost the last shot fired, but lived on until he was eighty-five years old. The column was designed by Thomas Harrison, the Chester architect, and the bronze statue was added in 1860, following the death of Uxbridge who had by then become the first Marquess of Anglesey following his brave exploits on the battlefield.

The tower of Moelfre limestone has an internal staircase of one hundred and fifteen steps. The view from the platform is a breath-taking panorama of the Strait from end to end, set against the dramatic back-cloth of Snowdonia *(Eryri)* and is a popular attraction with visitors to the island.

Below Saint Mary's Church, Llanfair Pwllgwyngyll, on the shore close to Britannia Bridge *(Pont Britannia)* stands another, smaller statue. This is of Horatio Nelson, and was erected as a navigational aid in 1873 by Admiral Lord Clarence Paget, the fourth son of the first Marquess. He was commander in chief of the Mediterranean fleet. His home was the nearby grey mansion of Plas Llanfair.

After Paget's death in 1895 Plas Llanfair had several owners. It was used as a family home and, for some years, as a hotel. The Haigh-Wood family who used it as a summer home had a daughter, Vivienne, who was the first wife of the poet, T.S. Eliot.

Latterly, Plas Llanfair became the *Indefatigable*, a training establishment which aimed to prepare boys for life in the merchant navy. The first *Indefatigable*, founded in 1864 by John Clift with a group of Liverpool ship-owners, was a fifty-gun frigate anchored in the River Mersey. When this was condemned as unfit in 1912, the school moved to a cruiser called *Phaeton* berthed at Rock Ferry. The boys were evacuated to a disused holiday camp on the northern Wales coast during the Second World War. Three years later Plas Llanfair was bought. The school remained here until 1995, when it was forced into liquidation due to a combination of rising costs and a dwindling British mercantile fleet. A stained glass window in Saint Mary's church, where the boys attended church parade, pictures the development of the school from its early days.

Plas Llanfair was then sold again, this time to the Ministry of Defence. A special charity supporting the armed services donated over £1m to develop a self-catering holiday complex known as a Joint Services Mountain Training Centre. It has a sailing club with resident instructor, a climbing wall and a small indoor swimming pool. Members of the three armed services and their families now use the facilities at minimal cost. But the link with *Indefatigable* remains in the name of the centre, and in the ship's bell since bought at auction by the Marine Engineers Guild of Liverpool and returned to Plas Llanfair.

The small creek where the boundary of Plas Llanfair land meets the wall of the Plas Newydd estate and where Afon Braint tumbles into the Strait, is Pwllfanogl, at one time a busy little port with cottages and small industries. The creek is well sheltered and an ideal place for small ships to anchor. Ships called on their return voyage to Liverpool after delivering goods to Caernarfon and Felinheli, taking on board school slates and slate pencils made in the small factory near the waterside.

Coal was delivered here, too, for distribution by horse and cart to the surrounding farms and villages. Ships would have the expert guidance of a pilot stationed along the coast and working between his home and Menai Bridge *(Porthaethwy)* to steer them safely through the dangerous waters of the Strait.

A map of 1862 shows Pwllfanogl to have had a flour mill, several storehouses, over a dozen cottages and houses with their pig styes, a public house called *The Pilot Boat*, and a cookshop. Later it was to have margarine and bacon factories and a building to dry and roast chicory.

The Menai Strait hereabouts has a deep pool which is the resting-place of an important wreck found during a marine biological survey. This was a chance find, as the wreck had blended with the seabed and was covered with large rocks which, over time, had fallen in to the water and sunk to the bottom. The survey brought to light interesting information. It suggested that the ship was loaded with over forty-eight thousand slates, some twenty tons in all. These were what was known as *singles* in the industry, a general purpose slate quarried until about 1740.

The vessel was clinker-built, fifteen metres long and a little over four metres across the beam. The hull was of oak and the timbers were cleaved, not sawn. It has been proved that the boat was built in the medieval tradition of boat building, and a radio carbon date on a sample of timber puts it in the 17th century. Experts say that the vessel sank between 1570 and 1690.

Today all is quiet at Pwllfanogl. The industries have disappeared and so have some of the cottages. But one or two remain. In one lives Sir Kyffin Williams, the Royal Academician whose portraits and landscapes enjoy huge popularity at home and abroad.

From Plas Newydd to Moel-y-don

The hamlet of Pwllfanogl nestles beside the wall which surrounds the Plas Newydd estate. The mansion of Plas Newydd, home to Marquesses of Anglesey and their forbears from the 16th century, stands in a magnificent position in full view from the Strait. It presents a dramatic picture in the autumn as the creeper partly covering it changes colour from green to brilliant red, and the trees take on their autumn colours.

The precise date of the first house on the site is not known, but it was Sir Nicholas Bayly, second Baronet (1707-1782) who made the first extensive alterations and the house began to look as it appears today. Sir Nicholas's son, who had also inherited the barony of Paget and was later to become Earl of Uxbridge, altered the building again. In 1793 he commissioned James Wyatt and Joseph Potter as his architects.

The most famous Earl of Uxbridge, undoubtedly, was Henry Paget who fought at the Battle of Waterloo, where he lost a leg. His exploits are chronicled in the military museum at Plas Newydd and he is remembered by the Anglesey Column referred to previously. In recognition of his bravery while serving as second in command to Wellington, he was created first Marquess of Anglesey. The present Marquess is the seventh. He and the Marchioness continue to live at Plas Newydd, although they have gifted the property to the National Trust.

The shore between Pwllfanogl and the house is a rhododendron garden of note. Planting was begun by the 6th Marquess but came to a standstill during the Second World War. More rigorous and planned planting began again when the present Marquess married. The second Lord Aberconway presented Lord Anglesey with a collection of 'thinnings' from the famous rhododendrons at Bodnant as a wedding present, and encouraged him to revive the garden by ensuring that each year from 1948 to 1951 a consignment of plants was delivered to Plas Newydd in the care of two gardeners to plant them. The rhododendron walk is now a special feature of the park, with many visitors from all over the world coming especially to view the display in season.

The gardens and park at Plas Newydd were designed by Humphry Repton in 1798-99, whose *Red Book* (so called because of its red cover) containing details of the original design still exists. Two world wars halted developments during the twentieth century but the present Marquess, a military historian, is also a keen gardener and his enthusiasm continues to be reflected in additions made since the 1940s.

The Italianate garden on the north side of the house, slightly elevated, has stunning views across the Strait. It was created by the 6th Marquess, designed on the foundations of an Edwardian conservatory. Recent re-designing has included an attractive trickling water feature surrounded by ferns. The wide herbaceous borders fringing the lower terrace are a wash of blue in summer with stately *agapanthus*.

Hidden behind the terrace, its roof top only discernible from the water when the surrounding trees are not in leaf, is the building erected to house the *Conway* school after the ship was wrecked. This, known now as the Conway Centre, is used for training in outdoor pursuits, as is part of the house known as the Nelson Centre, where young people from schools in Wales and beyond come to perfect their skills in sailing and outdoor activities.

Originally the main drive to Plas Newydd from the road swept down through the park to the main entrance of the house which was then facing the Strait. But access was altered when later structural alterations were made. What an impression guests to Plas Newydd received in those days as they bowled along in their carriages to be faced, suddenly, with the glorious view over the water as they drew up to the entrance.

Gardens to the south-west are a picture at every season with magnolias, azaleas and other spring flowering shrubs making springtime a season to remember especially. From the water, the borders of *hydrangeas* and great hedges of *potentilla* make a colourful summer frame to the house.

Anglesey *(Ynys Môn)* is noted for its ancient monuments. Standing stones, burial chambers and hut circles are all evidence of life and death on the island centuries ago. The Neolithic civilisation (2500-1900 BC) is represented by the great megaliths used to build tombs. Settlements appeared in the coastal areas where settlers could find food more easily, and fish. Two burial chambers can still be seen on the Plas Newydd estate, one on the slope behind the house as one looks from the water, and the other, Bryn yr Hen Bobl, on estate farmland nearby.

Bryn yr Hen Bobl was first excavated in 1929. Finds have included pottery, axes, scrapers of flint, a large locally quarried grit hone on which stone axes were sharpened and polished, animal and human bones, shells and charcoal. Close by are the remains of a terrace of huts.

The small promontory called Moel-y-don, west of the park, where today's visitors park their cars to relax and admire the view across to Felinheli, was once a small but busy boat-building yard, building vessels of around one hundred tons. Today barely anything remains but the bare bones of a boat, lapped by the tide.

One of the six ferries operating across the Strait worked from Moel-y-don to Felinheli. This was especially busy on Monday mornings and Saturdays, taking quarrymen whose homes were in the Llanidan district to and from their work in the Dinorwig slate quarries at Llanberis. It was regarded as one of the safest ferry crossings. John Wesley, on his forays into Anglesey *(Ynys Môn)* is said to have used it twice.

The prominent church spire behind the shoreline is that of Saint Edwen's church, Llanedwen. This church was almost completely rebuilt in 1856, the only remaining masonry from the previous building on the site being incorporated in the lower part of the west wall. According to local historian Henry Rowlands, Saint Edwen founded her cell here in AD 640. Some of the gravestones and the church furnishings date from the 15th and 17th centuries. Llanedwen church is the only church in Wales in regular use to be lit entirely by candles.

There are several graves of old retainers of the Anglesey *(Ynys Môn)* family from Plas Newydd in the churchyard, where they lie close to those of their employers, earlier Marquesses. Henry Rowlands, environmentalist, cleric and historian is buried at Llanedwen. His is best known for his book, *Mona Antiqua Restorata*, published in 1723. He was born nearby at Plas Gwyn, Llanedwen, and was ordained deacon in Bangor. In 1682 he was given the living of Llanfairpwll and Llantysilio, later becoming vicar of Llanidan, Llanedwen, Llanddaniel-fab and Llanfair-yn-y-cwmwd. He and his wife brought up twelve children.

In 1704 Henry Rowlands wrote an essay on agriculture in Anglesey *(Ynys Môn)* in which he advocated the use of sand and rotted seashells as fertilisers, and stressed the importance of providing adequate shelter for cattle and crops on this windy island. The veracity of some of his claims is now doubted, but nevertheless Henry Rowlands' writings are valuable as an indication of the agricultural state of the island during his lifetime and the developing interest of a local researcher who, as well as being personally interested, was invited to comment by the curator of the Ashmolean Museum in Oxford, Edward Lluyd, on the natural history of his parishes. Oxford was merely a place-name to Henry Rowlands. He never visited England.

A few hundred metres from the shore at Moel-y-don, sheltered from the water by a band of trees, stands Plas Coch, an attractive stepped-gabled 16th century house, now the hub of a caravan park. This was built by David Lloyd ap Hugh in 1569. It is a three-storeyed house of red sandstone with a slated roof. The Hughes family of Plas Coch was one of the famous

Anglesey *(Ynys Môn)* county families of the 16th and early 17th centuries, but even before the Act of Union those who lived in 'Porthamel Isa' as the house was then called had some connection with the legal administration of Anglesey *(Ynys Môn)*.

David's son, Hugh Hughes, studied at Lincoln's Inn in 1571 and became Queen's Attorney in North Wales in 1596. Between 1580 and 1600 he represented Anglesey *(Ynys Môn)* in Parliament and was Sheriff three times. Towards the end of the century Hugh Hughes reconstructed Plas Coch, adding the imposing square tower. He reached the peak of his career when he was sworn a member of the Council of the Marches in 1602. In 1609 King James sanctioned his appointment as Lord Chief Justice of Ireland, but Hugh Hughes died in June of that year, before he could assume office.

Moel-y-don to Llanddwyn

The Anglesey *(Ynys Môn)* shore at the western end of the Menai Strait is a quiet stretch of low-lying green fields, sandbanks and rabbit warren.

This area saw the invasion of the island by Suetonius Paulinus in AD61 and Julius Agricola in AD76, when Roman forces were out to destroy Druidism. Tacitus, recording the action, describes how they mustered on the mainland to be faced by a battle-line of men brandishing weapons, interspersed by shrieking women carrying torches, and Druids invoking their Gods. The Roman officers ordered their men across in a flotilla of flat-bottomed boats. The Druids put up no resistance and were massacred. In spite of this initial Roman foray, Suetonius Paulinus did not colonise Môn but left it to Agricola to do so several years later.

Some four hundred yards from the coast, barely seen from the water, stand the ruins of Llanidan Church. A 14th century doorway remained after the demolition in 1844, when the whole of the eastern part of the church with the exception of an arcade disappeared. When the modern parish church at Brynsiencyn was built, some fittings were moved there from Llanidan including bells from the first half of the 14th century and of the late 15th century. The strangely top-heavy tower of the newer church can be seen across the fields, at the entrance to Brynsiencyn village.

Further west, a minor road leads down from there to a cluster of cottages on the sea-shore at Barras. At one time this was a busy crossing place to Caernarfon, from Y Foel. These days the road is used by visitors making for the Anglesey Sea Zoo.

The shore road is a pleasant promenade in the summer. In the winter it can be windswept and inhospitable, and is left to the sea birds.

The complex of white buildings across a field houses the

Anglesey Sea Zoo, one of the island's most popular tourist attractions. This highly successful project was set up by David and Alison Lea-Wilson, two ex-Bangor University graduates. Beginning as oyster farmers and fish merchants along with a third partner in 1983, the Sea Zoo developed through their combined interest in marine biology and handling live oysters and lobsters before selling on the open market. More money was invested, and by 1994 they had ceased to be fish merchants. David and Alison then bought out their partner.

The Sea Zoo provides a fascinating insight into the teeming life of the sea. Tanks are fed by sea water. Conservation is high on the list of priorities here, and the aim is to present glimpses of offshore life in as natural surroundings as possible.

Diversifying, David and Alison Lea-Wilson established Cwmni Halen Môr Môn – The Anglesey Sea Salt Company – which produces high quality, gourmet standard white-flaked salt which is harvested from the water around the island, and sold through a number of independent retailers ranging from a small but distinctive Beaumaris shop to Fortnum & Mason in London. The owners are looking to expand their salt business, as demand almost outstrips production.

The Sea Zoo remains open throughout the year, and is upgraded continuously with emphasis on customer care, conservation and breeding projects.

Here the Strait is over a mile wide. The first passenger ferry service from Tal-y-foel to Caernarfon sailed in 1425. It was then leased to private individuals. It plied across a very exposed area of the Strait. Records show that in later years passengers had to be carried ashore on the backs of the ferrymen, as the shifting sands of Traeth Gwyllt made this crossing hazardous. In 1849 a 75 foot (23m) long steamboat, the *Menai* sailed between Y Foel and Caernarfon and the service appears to have been successful for a time. But the sandbank of Traeth Gwyllt remained a problem for the functioning of a ferry service despite building a pier at Y Foel to accommodate boats at low water.

One of the physical features of south-west Anglesey, instantly noticeable on the O.S. map, is the hooked spit of land which has the dramatic effect of almost closing the western extremity of the Strait at Abermenai. This is the result of tidal currents over the centuries, which still flow with a velocity of up to five knots in the narrows between Abermenai Point and the opposite mainland shore at Belan.

The extensive sandbanks of Traeth Melynog and Traeth Gwyllt lie between Y Foel and the spit, penetrated by channels which end blindly in the sand flats. The Abermenai spit runs for almost 2 miles (3.2km) from the dunes at Newborough *(Niwbwrch)*. Nearest the shore it consists of a series of dune ridges running north-eastwards to the sand flats of Traeth Melynog. This section is followed by a narrow length consisting of a single sand ridge, the weakest part of the spit which has been breached a number of times by the sea in rough weather. Protective work has been, and continues to be carried out to maintain the contour of the land. The outer section of the spit is higher, and has maintained its hooked shape for centuries. All the Admiralty charts and large scale O.S. maps of the past two hundred years show the hook in its present form.

Writing in the Transactions of the Anglesey Antiquarian Society in 1980, A.H.W. Robinson comments, 'Historical evidence indicates that it must have existed in much its present form for at least seven hundred years, for when the officials of Edward I visited the area prior to the building of Caernarfon castle shortly after 1285 they named the feature South Crook, a reference to the hooked appearance of the spit as it appeared when sailing through the narrow entrance into the Menai Strait'.

Edward was to create a settlement at Rhosyr in 1303, when he moved nearly all the population of Llanfaes to enable him to site his castle at Beaumaris. The new market town was called Newborough *(Niwbwrch)*. For forty years it was the seat of the county court.

A ferry crossed to the mainland from Abermenai, but was

not popular as no proper road was ever made to it, the passengers needing to travel to and from it on horseback. It is best remembered for the large boat which took people from this corner of Anglesey *(Ynys Môn)* to Caernarfon on market days. In 1725 Daniel Defoe used the Abermenai ferry on his way to Holyhead *(Caergybi)* but in December 1785 the ferry boat sank. Over fifty passengers lost their lives.

Shifting sand from Caernarfon Bay has formed Newborough Warren, one of the finest dunelands in Wales. Once the area had more fields than exist today but in the 14th century huge storms blew sand inland and these fields were inundated to form the Newborough *(Niwbwrch)* dunes. As there were no trees or bushes to hold back the sand, it quickly engulfed farmland and homesteads. Eleven cottages were overwhelmed by these and later violent storms, and the remains, known as *Hendai*, can be seen in the forest today. The Warren is now in the care of the Countryside Council for Wales.

Land usage in the warren dates from the Middle Ages and included rabbit farming, marram grass mat-making and wool processing. Rabbits, introduced by the Normans to provide food, are known to have been taken commercially from Newborough *(Niwbwrch)* since the 13th century. During the Second World War, Newborough *(Niwbwrch)* like other sand dune systems in Britain, was used as a bombing and rifle range. After the war about half the site, 2,000 acres, was planted with trees, mainly Corsican pine, with a view to stabilising the system, producing timber, and providing employment. This part is now cared for by the Forestry Commission. In 1955 the eastern half of the dune system was created a Site of Special Scientific Interest (SSSI).

The warren duneland is crossed by paths, Llwybr y Twyni and Llwybr Penlon. Llwybr y Braint leads partly across the sands to Abermenai Point. Paths also exist through the wooded areas.

The vast stretch of Llanddwyn Bay to the west of the spit

culminates in Llanddwyn island. It is estimated that over 250,000 people visit Llanddwyn beach each year to enjoy sea, sunshine and the extensive views across to the mountains of Llŷn. Ten thousand make the mile and a half walk across the beach to Llanddwyn island, to visit the cottages and take in the romantic story of Saint Dwynwen.

Dwynwen was the daughter of the chieftain, Brychan, who gave his name to Brycheiniog according to some traditions. She built an oratory on Llanddwyn island in the 5th century when she sought solitude after a broken love affair. This, it was claimed, caused the waters of a nearby well to take on miraculous powers which enabled lovers to determine the faithfulness of their sweethearts. Tradition had it that if a few crumbs of fresh wheaten bread, sprinkled on the water, were covered with a cloth, the sacred eel would then appear in the water. If the cloth was disturbed and sank, the lover would be faithless. Visitors placed offerings at the shrine of the saint.

In later years a church was erected on the site of the cell and by the time Henry VIII came to the throne, this had become one of the richest churches in the Bangor diocese. A cross commemorating Saint Dwynwen was raised in 1897 close to the lighthouse.

By 1840 there was a lifeboat stationed at Pilot's Cove, the coxswain living in a nearby cottage. The crew lived at Newborough (Niwbwrch) three and a half miles away, and they were signalled by firing a cannon when they were needed to go out to a ship in distress.

In 1845 the light called Tŵr Mawr was built. It had a curved glass window and was lit by an oil lamp backed by reflectors and fronted by a sheet of red glass. Two more cottages were added and Llanddwyn became the pilot station for ships travelling along the buoyed channel to Caernarfon.

There are many wrecks along this coast. In 1840 a full-rigged ship, Mountaineer was sailing from the Spanish Main to Liverpool when she was lost during a storm. All the crew, except for one boy, were saved. The ship broke up, but the figurehead, which was washed ashore, was rescued and taken to the mainland where it was displayed in a house for many years. Another ship, the *Monk* sailed from Porthdin-llaen to Liverpool with a cargo of pigs. The ship was wrecked near an offshore island which was afterwards referred to as 'Craig y Mochyn' *(pig rock)*.

Llanddwyn to Bodorgan

Maintenance of a sensitive and apparently mobile site such as Newborough Warren calls for the closest co-operation of all the bodies involved, in order to keep the fine line between stabilisation, and over-stabilisation which could destroy a natural phenomenon. Marram grass was one means of stabilising the dunes. Queen Elizabeth I prohibited the cutting of marram grass in the area immediately around Newborough *(Niwbwrch)* but supplies could be harvested from the common land on the Warren. The people of Newborough *(Niwbwrch)* took advantage of this free material to create a cottage industry to make mats, baskets and ropes. This was carried on over a long period.

The Enclosures Acts put land into the hands of private owners who began to charge for harvesting the grass, and eventually rented out plots to cottagers. Women worked at home, plaiting the mats which were sold to farmers for covering haystacks. The ropes tying them down were also made from the grass. Nets were made for trapping rabbits. The men made brooms and besoms and these, along with kneeling mats, floor mats, mattresses and baskets were bartered for goods or sold at the local fairs.

The bartering system came to an end in the early 20th century when the *Newborough Mat Makers Association* was set up under the initiative of local entrepreneur Col. Stapleton-Cotton (who also had a hand in setting up the Women's Institute movement in Britain). By the 1930s, demand had diminished, skills had disappeared, and today the craft of mat-making from marram grass has become an art form.

Beyond the tree plantation of the Warren lies the wide expanse of the Cefni estuary. At one time the sea almost reached Llangefni at high tide, a distance of twelve miles from the coast.

The land around the river was marshland, and difficult to

cross in most weathers. The Malltraeth and Corsddegau Marsh Act of 1788 initiated a scheme of drainage and work was begun in 1790. But problems arose when building the Cob which was intended to hold back the sea, owing to damage done by high tides. A new act was necessary to give the commissioners greater power to enforce contributions from the owners of the land.

The intention of the scheme was to build an embankment of furze faggots bound with double cordage which would be covered with sand and sods. There would be a stone pavement on the seaward side. The Cob was to be 1400 yards (1280m) long, 50 yards (46m) wide at the base and 4 yards (3.7m) wide at the top, and 5 yards (4.6m) high. It was a considerable undertaking. Work started from both sides at the same time, and the two halves would be joined in the middle where the force of water would be greatest.

By January 1796 it was almost complete, when an unusually high tide breached the embankment and work was halted. The cost until then had been £12,000. The breach remained for several years until, in 1811, a third Act was passed to increase the powers of the two previous ones, and when completed the total cost was in the region of £50,000.

The final stage of the work, filling the central breach, was the most difficult. This was done by bringing an old hulk from Caernarfon, jamming it into the space and filling it with rubble. By 1812 the Cob was complete, and a roadway was constructed between Malltraeth and Newborough (Niwbwrch) which allowed local farmers from this side of Anglesey (Ynys Môn) to take their produce to the Menai ferries for sale in Caernarfon market, whatever the state of the weather or the tide.

Draining the marsh was another considerable feat, as the course of Afon Cefni had to be altered. This was done by channelling it in a straight line, with high embankments on each side. The original intention was that it should be navigable.

A small coalfield on the marsh worked to provide fuel for the copper industry at Amlwch. Malltraeth Yard, as the village was then called, was a busy little port and shipbuilding yard.

Today the crest of the Cob provides a delightful raised walk where visitors can enjoy wide views and wild life. The land immediately below on the landward side is a nature reserve, its brackish pools and grassland home to many unusual species of plants and flowers and the haunt of birds. The acres now drained by the channelled river have provided valuable grazing land. It has been estimated that 1470 acres of land were improved.

The village of Malltraeth sits comfortably on the sandy shore, with a straggle of houses reaching out towards the sea. In one of these houses, during the 1940s to 1979, lived Charles Tunnicliffe, Royal Academician and illustrator of over eighty countryside books.

Charles Tunnicliffe was born in 1901, the son of a Cheshire farmer. He and his artist wife, Winifred, moved from Macclesfield to Malltraeth in 1947, when he had already made a name for himself in bird portraiture. The couple chose to live at 'Shorelands', where he could look out on to the estuary and study and draw birds. His preliminary sketches which he called his *bird books* reflect the hours he spent in patient study. His scraper-board drawings and fresh paintings have an attraction all their own, and are a lively record of his field studies, mostly on the Cefni estuary at Malltraeth. Since his death in 1979, by which time he was almost blind and unable to see to paint, his pictures have become increasingly valuable.

Oriel Ynys Môn at Llangefni has reproduced a corner of his studio at 'Shorelands' in its permanent exhibition hall, an evocative re-creation where the visitor can look out beyond his drawing board at the wide view of the estuary from which he gained inspiration for his work. The gallery now holds the major collection of his drawings and paintings.

Bodorgan Hall, the home of the Meyrick family for

centuries, is little known by Anglesey *(Ynys Môn)* residents or tourists, as it stands well away from the passing road in a superb position above the mile (1.6km) wide Cefni estuary with panoramic views across to the Newborough Forest and the mountains beyond. It is a private family home of the Meyrick family, and not open to the public.

The present 18th century house is not the original dwelling. When Owen Meyrick, barrister-at-law and member of Parliament for the county of Anglesey, died in 1770 the estate passed to his son, Owen Putland Meyrick, who was eighteen years old and a student at Oxford. He lived in London after graduating, married into money, and spent little time at Bodorgan although he had been made High Sheriff in 1774. It was not until 1779 that he began to plan changes at his seat in Anglesey *(Ynys Môn)*.

The Meyrick family socialised with the Bulkeleys of Beaumaris and no doubt this is where Owen came to know John Cooper, assistant and clerk of works to Samuel Wyatt who was then remodelling the Bulkeley mansion of Baron Hill. Owen commissioned Cooper to re-build Bodorgan Hall.

Records of the re-building tell how the old house was demolished at a cost of £26.5s.0d. Prices of materials for the new work are quoted. Whereas most of the materials used to build the old hall would have been obtained locally, much of those necessary for the new hall, especially timber, was imported from Liverpool merchants. In the winter months ships had to contend with the weather in Liverpool Bay, and when they did finally arrive at the port of Beaumaris some way had to be found to transport the goods across country to Bodorgan. It all cost money, and progress was slow.

A new quarry was opened not far from the house. The stone extracted was found to be of excellent quality and there was plenty to be had, so this was used for the external walls of the house.

Unlike many absentee estate owners, Owen Putland

Meyrick was keenly interested in the progress of building his new house, and there is evidence in the records of his many visits. He plagued his architect over small details, and some of the letters from Cooper to his patron, commenting on his suggestions, carry an undertone of politely veiled frustration. The domestic block was finished first, and Meyrick used what was to be the housekeeper's room when he chose to make his frequent visits.

Progress was erratic. Bad weather held up work. There was sickness among the workers and the quarry flooded. There were disputes among the workmen. There was a long disagreement between Meyrick and Cooper about the style of windows to be installed. But eventually the work was completed, and in 1784 it was said that Bodorgan Hall could vie with any newly built house in northern Wales. In the course of three and a half years John Cooper had replaced Owen Meyrick's 17th century home with an elegant neo-classical house which still retains Cooper's original design features.

Bodorgan to Rhosneigr

The windswept sand dunes of the Bodowen and Trefri Warrens carry the coastline around from the point at Pen y Parc to Aberffraw.

Tywyn Aberffraw, crossed by the metalled road from Malltraeth, is a spectacular and scientifically interesting common, still grazed to some extent over the more established dunes now covered with grass. Botanists enthuse over wild thyme and ladies' bedstraw, sand sedge and several species of ferns. Wander only a short distance from the road and civilisation, and one is in another world, alone among undulating mounds of sand separated by dune pools or slacks.

Where Afon Ffraw meets the sea, a broad bank of firmer sand fringes the common. This is Traeth Mawr, the venue for holidaymakers who leave their cars by the road and carry beach paraphernalia along the river, to spend the day on the shore in the sunshine.

It is difficult to realise that the little village of Aberffraw was one of the most important places in northern Wales, when it was the seat of the Princes of Gwynedd. The last traces of an early court have disappeared, but Llywelyn ap Iorwerth's name is perpetuated in Llys Llywelyn, a group of restored farm buildings in the centre of the village, now used as a Coastal Heritage Centre. The Centre has meeting rooms, a library, and exhibitions by various bodies concerned with the countryside and archaeological conservation. Summer courses and walks are organised. This is also the base from which professional and volunteer workers go out to conserve footpaths, and plant the dunes to battle against sand invasion.

The tiny hump-backed bridge crossing Afon Ffraw at the entrance to the village is now by-passed, but remains a favourite subject with photographers. It was built in 1731, and is one of the few bridges in Anglesey *(Ynys Môn)* that can be dated.

Like Malltraeth and many of the coastal villages of Anglesey *(Ynys Môn)*, Aberffraw once had its shipbuilding yard.

Leaving Aberffraw, the shore becomes rocky and is dotted with small islands. One of these, at Porth Cwyfan, stands some two hundred yards from high watermark. A small, squat church perches above the water, surrounded by a wall. This is Llangwyfan, one of Anglesey's earliest religious sites. The present church dates back to the 12th century, although there was a religious cell here five centuries before. At one time a causeway led to the island, and services were held regularly. If the causeway was impassable because of abnormally high tides or stormy weather, the service would be held in a consecrated room at nearby Plas Llangwyfan. Most of the causeway has now disappeared, and reaching the island can be an adventure, especially when attempting to beat the tide. The church was repaired in 1893 and occasionally services are held there during the summer.

In days gone by the officiating parson could claim 'hay for his horse, two eggs for his breakfast, a penny loaf and half a pint of small beer' from Plas Llangwyfan farm.

The south-western corner of Anglesey *(Ynys Môn)* has been notorious for shipwrecks. As recently as 1938 the coasting steamer *Kyle Prince* was carrying cement from Barry to Liverpool and ran into trouble near Ynys Enlli *(Bardsey Island)* off the Llŷn peninsula, when a circulatory pipe leading to the engine room broke. While engineers struggled to repair it, the stokehold flooded and huge waves crashed into the engine room, the water dowsing the furnaces. Calls for help brought no response, and gales blew the ship towards the Anglesey *(Ynys Môn)* coast as she sank lower into the water. Eventually the Holyhead *(Caergybi)* lifeboat reached the *Kyle Prince* and took off the crew. Although by this time the ship was anchored, the cables snapped and she was driven on to the rocks at Caethle, where the waves smashed her to pieces.

In the 18th and 19th centuries stealing from wrecks along

this coast was rife, although it was considered a serious crime and the consequences could be very unpleasant if the miscreants were caught and convicted. In 1823 the *Flora* was lost with all hands off Aberffraw. Two men found guilty of stealing flotsam were not only imprisoned for six months, but, on their release, were publicly flogged at Aberffraw where a large crowd turned out to witness the event.

Rounding Ynys Meibion and the now redundant army training area above Caethle, the next bay is Porth Trecastell – Cable Bay to tourists. When electric telegraph systems came into operation in the 1850s several abortive attempts were made to link the north-western corner of Anglesey *(Ynys Môn)* with Ireland, the first being a cable weighing one ton per mile laid by the steamship *Britannia* from Holyhead to Dublin in sixteen days. All the attempts failed for various reasons, and it was decided to try a landing farther south. Finally the successful link was made between Dublin and Porth Trecastell.

A grassy path leads from the beach car park over the headland to one of the most important archaeological sites in Wales. *Barclodiad y Gawres* is a neolithic burial chamber complex which has been heavily restored. Sir Mortimer Wheeler, the archaeologist who became so well known through his television appearances, was involved. Some five thousand years ago men carved spirals, zig-zags and chevrons to decorate their stone tombs and these can be seen here. The style is similar to that seen in the famous Irish tombs at Newgrange.

Beyond Barclodiad y Gawres, the village of Rhosneigr lies on the shore, with Llyn Maelog between the railway and the sea. An ordnance survey map of the late 1800s shows Rhosneigr as a coastguard station, with a dozen or so houses, a chapel and a hotel scattered over the common. The hotel – the Maelog Hotel – was built on the dunes in 1863 by Evan Thomas of Liverpool, one of the famous family of bonesetters of whom we shall hear more later. He had bought the rights to the common from the Department of Woods and Forests. Local people objected as they could see their rights to graze cattle usurped, but were assured by Evan Thomas that they would be respected.

At that time the temperance movement had a strong following in Anglesey *(Ynys Môn)* and sympathisers objected vociferously to a hotel where strong drink would be sold. But work began in spite of their objections, a guard being set up each evening to be on the lookout for trouble. A crowd gathered near the site in October 1863, and one of those guards was severely manhandled and thrown into the lake, the mob blowing up the partially built hotel. Seventeen of the objectors were jailed as a result. The hotel was completed eventually, proving a great attraction for the newly developing seaside resort.

As seaside holidays became more popular Rhosneigr attracted city dwellers looking for sandy beaches, rocky pools, wide views, fresh air and the opportunity for relaxation in pleasant surroundings. A station was provided on the existing railway line. Llyn Maelog offered fishing, and its reed beds gave nature lovers a unique opportunity to study wild life.

Developers saw their opportunity to build houses and guest houses. Soon Rhosneigr became a bustling little holiday resort in the summer, with spasmodic, rather untidy and sometimes hastily erected development providing accommodation for tourists. Artists came to set up their studios in the village. George Cockram, the Birkenhead artist famed for his local studies and paintings of the Conwy valley was one of them.

Rhosneigr had a brief burst of glory in 1930 when the great airship, *R101*, was seen over the village. The mother of the pilot, Lt Commander Irwin, lived in Rhosneigr, and the skies over Anglesey *(Ynys Môn)* in those days being comparatively free of aircraft, the pilot decided to 'visit' to show off his wonderful flying machine to his proud parent.

There was a lifeboat station at Rhosneigr from 1872 to 1924. During the course of twenty-nine active service launches, seventy-three lives were saved.

One of the most famous shipwrecks which demonstrated the bravery of lifeboat crews was that of the *Norman Court* which sank in Cymyran Bay, not far from Rhosneigr. In March 1883 the barque, which was over one hundred days out of Surabaya in Java with a cargo of sugar, bound for Greenock, was driven ashore by a strong gale. Two of the twenty-two crew died after a horrendous experience of a night spent in the ship's mizzen rigging. The crews of Rhosneigr and Holyhead lifeboats went to the rescue. The Holyhead crew was towed in the lifeboat to the north-west of South Stack, then sailed to a position off Cymyran Bay, to be towed by a tug to within a mile of the wreck. Their final approach was made in mountainous seas under oars. Three attempts in two hours failed, and the lifeboat had to return to Holyhead *(Caergybi)*.

The Rhosneigr lifeboat made attempts to save the men from under the jib boom of the *Norman Court*, and from the shore, again unsuccessfully. Meanwhile the Holyhead crew, who were all experienced seamen, were put on a special train from Holyhead *(Caergybi)* to Rhosneigr and went out in the Rhosneigr lifeboat. They managed to rescue all the surviving crew. The Holyhead men received R.N.L.I. awards in recognition of their extreme persistence and bravery.

Afon Crigyll enters the sea to the north of Rhosneigr after flowing through marsh and dunes. This area, and the practice of enticing ships to their doom by hanging lighted lamps around the necks of grazing cattle to simulate undulating ships' lights in harbour, before plundering the wrecks, inspired a local lawyer, W.D. Owen, to write a novel based on the time of the Civil Wars, which he called *Madam Wen*.

This practice was called Cornish Lamping. Lewis Morris, customs officer at Holyhead *(Caergybi)* wrote in 1741 to the Admiralty that 'false charts serve but as false lights laid by villains along ye coast to lead poor sailors to destruction'. Writing in the Anglesey Antiquarian Society's Transactions of 1974, Captain Geoffrey Butterworth, a seasoned mariner himself, commented:

It is tempting to suppose that false compasses aided ill-done coastal surveys and Cornish Lamping to pile these wrecks at Cymyran, but ships at that time had wooden timbers and the complete absence of lighthouses was probably more important'.

Madam Wen was first serialised in weekly parts in a Welsh newspaper under the title *Madam Wen, Arwres yr Ogof* (Madam Wen, Heroine of the Cave). In 1925 it appeared as a book. The story tells of Einir Wyn, a beautiful woman who had lost her inheritance as a result of the Civil Wars and, as 'Madam Wen', led a group of thieves before falling in love with Morys Williams, the local squire. It has all the elements of romantic fiction, fast-moving action, murders, smugglers, the law, loves and hates and jealousies, with the action taking place in the lakeland area behind the wild western coast of Anglesey *(Ynys Môn)*.

Today Traeth Crigyll is hardly a quiet backwater. Jet aircraft and helicopters from R.A.F. Valley roar overhead.

Before the second world war, Tywyn Trewan, the extensive common north-west of Afon Crigyll, was a place for birds and grazing cattle. Had plans which were afoot in 1897 for an explosives works on fifty-five acres been allowed, it would have been very different. In 1941, R.A.F. Valley was built, then called R.A.F. Rhosneigr, and from 1943 to 1945 it was the transatlantic terminal of U.S.A.F. flights to Britain.

While extending the airfield in 1943, a magnificent collection of Celtic treasure was found during excavation work, including swords, spears, shield bosses and decorated bronze plaques. These were taken to Cardiff to be put in the safe keeping of the National Museum of Wales. One wonders if even more treasure lies hidden under R.A.F. Valley's tarmacadamed runways.

Rhosneigr to South Stack

The narrow strip of water separating Ynys Cybi *(Holy Island)* from the rest of Anglesey *(Ynys Môn)* crossed by Four Mile Bridge, is referred to locally as the Inland Sea. Sailing north-west up the coast of the island, the shore becomes increasingly rocky and precipitous, indented by small bays and fringed with tiny islets. The map marks Silver Bay, so called because of its clean, sandy beach; Borthwen (again, 'wen' in this context refers to its clean silver sand). Rhoscolyn beacon stands on Ynys y Gwylanod *(the island of gulls)*. Another rock in the sea is Maen y Frân *(Crow's Rock)*.

The shoreline to the Inland Sea is more gentle, with green fields down to the salt marsh. On the minor road south from Four Mile Bridge to the old house at Bodior is a worked-out quarry which, in its hey-day, produced the highly-prized Mona Green Marble. This stone was discovered at the end of the 18th century. The quarry was acquired by George Bullock, a furniture maker, in 1806. Bullock lived in Liverpool. where he began his career in cabinet making and general furnishing, and where he founded the Liverpool Academy.

One of his most prestigious pieces was a magnificent table fo green marble which was sent to Elba to be part of the furnishings of the 56-roomed bungalow which the British government built for Buonaparte while a prisoner. Bullock also used Mona Green Marble in fireplaces – one exists in a large house on the Menai Strait.

The church of Saint Gwenfaen, Rhoscolyn, stands a little way above the shore, at the confluence of minor roads. A church was established here in the 6th century. Although it was re-built between 1871 and 1879, baptisms are conducted at the 15th century font saved from the old church.

Saint Gwenfaen's well lies on the western slope of Rhoscolyn Head, a place of pilgrimage in centuries gone by when its waters were reputed to alleviate mental illness.

Pilgrims would throw two white spar stones in to the well, and if bubbles arose they expected a miracle.

At the end of the 19th century Rhoscolyn was the centre of a flourishing oyster fishery, but as the beds became overworked and exhausted, it declined.

This is a scattered community, somnolent out of season but pleasantly busy during the summer. There are some old cottages, now restored and updated and in use as holiday homes. In days gone by they housed workers at a china clay works and at a nearby quarry from which stone was quarried for the maintenance of Bristol, Peterborough and Worcester Cathedrals.

There are many pathways over Ynys Cybi *(Holy Island)*. One of the most popular with visitors is that from Rhoscolyn to Trearddur Bay along the cliff top. By the side of this path, opposite the sea-girt rock of Maen Piscar, is a small stone memorial to 'Tyger, September 17, 1819' which commemorates the devotion of a dog who helped to save the lives of four people following shipwreck.

This happened when a Liverpool-bound ketch struck Maen Piscar on a dark, foggy night. As the vessel sank Tyger, a retriever belonging to the captain, jumped into the sea and started to swim. His master, two sailors and a boy followed him, trusting in the dog's instinct to make for the shore, and Tyger eventually brought them to land. They were all exhausted but recovered, except for the faithful dog who licked the captain's hand and died.

The path gives dramatic views of the natural arches of Bwa Du and Bwa Wen, sculpted by time and the weather from remarkable cliff formations.

The west coast of Ynys Cybi *(Holy Island)* is battered by gales and mountainous seas in bad weather, so it is hardly surprising that a coastguard station was established at Rhoscolyn, and a lifeboat station by the Royal National Lifeboat Institution. A memorial at Rhoscolyn church commemorates the exploits of lifeboat crews. Between 1866 and 1881, they saved a hundred and two lives.

Like Rhosneigr, Trearddur has developed through the growing fashion for seaside holidays, and the existence of a beautiful natural bay. The old name for the village was Towyn y Capel, but the name of a nearby farm called Tre Arddur was adopted to distinguish it from another Towyn y Capel elsewhere.

There is an important medieval burial ground here which has been the subject of archaeological research within recent times. The site of a chapel to Saint Bride, it stands about twenty metres above high water mark in the bay with a frontage to the shore. Saint Ffraid is the patron saint of the present church. She was the saint traditionally believed to have arrived from Ireland floating on a sod.

Modern speculative development of housing more suited to an urban area has done nothing to enhance the beauty of Trearddur, which depends on the sea and the shore for its popularity.

A house called Towyn Lodge, on the southern approach to the village, was occupied by Thomas Telford while completing work on his London to Holyhead road. It is said he used the small tower in a corner of the garden overlooking Porth Diana as his workroom.

Ynys Cybi *(Holy Island)* is rich in burial mounds, chambers, standing stones, hut groups and hill forts, a veritable treasure island to those interested in life during the early occupation of Britain. A glance at the map will reveal their many locations. 'Cytiau'r Gwyddelod' *(Irishmen's huts)* refers to the remains of hut groups. This is perhaps a misnomer as there is no special Irish connection here. The Royal Commission for Ancient Monuments dates them to the late Stone Age.

Porth Dafarch, to the north of Trearddur Bay, became a harbour for the Irish Sea crossing to Dublin for one year, 1819-20. For sailing packets it provided an alternative to Holyhead

(Caergybi), giving more shelter in rough weather. A landing place was built and a new road to Holyhead *(Caergybi)* cut through the rock. But when steam took over from sail it was no longer needed so its importance was short-lived.

The four-masted screw barque, the *S.S. Missouri*, lies in pieces on the sea bed off Porth Dafarch. She was strongly built with seven bulkheads to withstand the Atlantic gales. In February 1886 *Missouri* was sailing from Boston in the United States to Liverpool with a mixed cargo of live cattle, hides, palm oil and cotton bales. A south-westerly gale blew the ship across Cardigan Bay in a dense fog and driving snowstorm. With visibility down to only a few yards, she struck the coast at Porth Dafarch on March 1st. The crew tried to lighten the load, unsuccessfully, by sending overboard a quarter of the three hundred and ninety-five cattle. Help was summoned. A cliff rescue team managed to haul ashore the ship's doctor, twenty eight cattlemen and three stowaways by means of a breeches buoy, leaving the captain and crew on board while tugs attempted to pull the ship off the rocks. By nightfall it was obvious that this was going to be impossible, and the crew had to abandon ship. Only fifty of the remaining cattle were saved.

Some of the cargo was later recovered, but explosives had to be used to blast a hole through the iron-plated hull and the ship finally broke up. But before she did so, looters were active and several men were tried and convicted for theft. After a month, the wreck was abandoned and broke up in later gales.

The wide bay north of Penrhyn Mawr is Abraham's Bosom, the graveyard of many ships wrecked in savage storms. A narrow minor road leads from Penrhosfeilw, high above Pen Las Rock, to one of Wales's most spectacularly situated lighthouses at South Stack. On the way is a small castellated turret – Elin's Tower. This was erected between 1820 and 1850 by the Stanley family of Penrhos, Holyhead *(Caergybi)* intended as a summer house. This area of coastal heath and cliffs is now a nature reserve and the Royal Society for the Protection of

Birds has taken over Elin's Tower to create an information centre and viewpoint.

Elin's Tower attracts more than thirty thousand visitors a year between April and September. The busiest time is during early summer when sea birds breed, and a view of thousands of birds on the cliffs can be had through the Society's fixed binoculars at the Tower. Guillemots, razorbills, puffins and gulls can all be seen jostling for precious nesting space on narrow ledges along the precipitous cliffs.

The coastline hereabouts is formed by massive granite cliffs rising sheer from the sea to a hundred and thirty five metres.

A petition for a patent to build a lighthouse at South Stack was first made to Charles II in 1665, but it was not until 1809 that the first light shone out from the rock. The lighthouse cost £12,000 to build. It was originally fitted with Argand oil lamps and reflectors. Fog often obscured the light so, to improve matters in 1840, a perpendicular rail was installed by means of which a lantern giving extra light could be lowered down to sea level.

During the mid 1870s the lantern and lighting apparatus was replaced by a new lantern. The year 1909 saw yet another replacement, this time with a more modern form of incandescent mantle burner, and in 1938 the station was electrified.

Keepers ceased to be employed in 1984 when the lighthouse was automated. The light and fog signal are now remotely controlled from the Trinity House Operational Control Centre at Harwich in Essex.

South Stack is a dramatic site, and access to it can be dangerous. The chasm between the mainland and the rock was first crossed by a hemp cable twenty one metres above sea level, along which a sliding basket was drawn carrying a passenger or stores. This was replaced in 1828 by a suspension bridge, and in 1964 by an aluminium bridge. The present footbridge was installed in 1997. The landward approach to the footbridge is made by descending four hundred steep steps cut into the cliff face.

The lighthouse and the island on which it stands was closed to the public for some years when it was realised that a new bridge was necessary to satisfy safety needs. It is now open again, but visits are by ticket only and strictly controlled. Public access is through a working partnership between Trinity House, the RSPB, the Countryside Council for Wales, and Ynys Môn County Council, with the financial help of the Welsh Development Agency.

Beyond South Stack, Gogarth Bay sweeps around the northernmost promontory of Ynys Cybi *(Holy Island)* North Stack. Here caves penetrate the cliffs. Parliament Cave is directly below the old fog signal station, a huge cavern so named because of the cacophony of sound from calling and chattering birds nesting there. The path to North Stack passes Caer y Twr, an ancient holl fort which covered seventeen acres. There was once a Roman warning beacon within the fort.

There are remains of a 19th century telegraph station above North Stack, the first in a line of eleven between Anglesey *(Ynys Môn)* and Liverpool, set up to give Liverpool merchants early warning of the approach of their ships to the port. The method used was semaphore. The operator at the North Stack station would pick up messages from ships at sea by flag, and relay these down the line by the wooden arms of the mast. The operators became so practised that it was claimed, on a clear day, that the first group of numbers carrying the coded message would have arrived in Liverpool by the time the last was leaving Holyhead, seventy-two miles away.

In days gone by life on Ynys Cybi *(Holy Island)* could be hard. For those living on the western rim of Anglesey *(Ynys Môn)*, the lighthouse keepers at South Stack or the signal operators at North Stack, it was solitary and, at times when the weather was at its worst, could be terrifying. Even the journey along the few miles down to Holyhead *(Caergybi)* could be

Afon Menai and the two bridges

Plas Newydd

Britannia Bridge over Afon
Menai now carries a highway
above the railway track.

The Marquess of Anglesey's
Column

Looking across Caernarfon Bay from Anglesey *(Ynys Môn)*.

Llanddwyn – an aerial view of the promontory

Bodorgan Hall

Aberffraw

Sunset over Llangwyfan church

Y Bwa Wen – a stone arch at Rhoscolyn

Remains of ancient forest, Trearddur Bay *(Bae Trearddur)*.

The rock coastline at Porth Dafarch which inspired the hymn
'Craig yr Oesedd' *(Rock of Ages)*.

South Stack Lighthouse, Holyhead *(Caergybi)*.

The inner harbour, Holyhead *(Caergybi)*.

Old Irish mail steamers at Holyhead *(Caergybi)*.

The Breakwater Quarry,
Holyhead*(Caergybi)*.

The Skerries Rock and
Lighthouse

The Bathing Creek, Amlwch

Llanbadrig church

Porth Amlwch

Porthwen brickworks

Old China Clay Works destroyed by fire 1920

Point Lynas (pilot boat jetty on right)

The main hut at Din Lligwy.

Moelfre

Traeth Benllech

The old harbour at Traeth Coch.

Ynys Seiriol *(Puffin Island)* from Penmon.

Penmon Priory

Beaumaris castle looking over Afon Menai
towards the Snowdonia stronghold

Beaumaris courthouse

Afon Menai is spanned by Telford's graceful suspension bridge.

fraught with danger.

People in the scattered communities lived a life apart. But all this was to change in the middle of the 19th century when the government decided a breakwater was necessary to create a new harbour at Holyhead *(Caergybi)*.

Holyhead (*Caergybi*)

One hundred and eighty years ago the port at Holyhead (*Caergybi*), which until then had been merely a creek, was about to be enlarged. Previously, if the tide was not appropriate for a safe berthing, passengers were carried to and from the ships on the backs of porters. From 1810 to 1824 the government spent £150,000 on improvements to facilitate the link between Holyhead and Ireland, and so encourage trade.

In 1810 it had been decided to build a pier from Salt Island. This was completed in 1821 and known as Admiralty Pier. A new Customs House and harbour office were built, and a graving dock said to be one of the first in Britain. An innovative feature of the harbour office was its clock tower, which showed the time on one face and the wind direction on another.

Holyhead (*Caergybi*) was considered to be a safe refuge in time of storm. In 1826 it was reported that more than a hundred and fifty sailing vessels sought its shelter in the course of a few days. It was becoming increasingly apparent that more shelter was needed for vessels which might otherwise be driven by storms on to a lee shore, and this shelter should be available where the frequency of shipwreck was the greatest.

Various plans were put forward by well-known engineers. Work began in January 1848 on the development designed by J.M. Rendel for a breakwater of 5,100 feet (1555m) from Soldier's Point out into the bay to end at Platters Buoy. From the eastern side of the bay it was intended to run a pier of 1200 feet (366m) from Salt Island. In all, 316 acres would be partially enclosed. The work would cost £700,000 and would result in one of the greatest harbours in the country.

It took twelve months to lay down a rail track from the quarry which was opened at Mynydd y Tŵr, the mountain behind the town. This was a broad gauge track built on stout wooden staging erected out to sea.

Stone from the new quarry was to provide the bulk of the

building material, with stone for the superstructure coming by sea from a quarry on the eastern coast of Anglesey (*Ynys Môn*).

Over a thousand men were employed on the project. More than forty lost their lives during construction between 1849 and 1852. Workers flocked to Holyhead (*Caergybi*), which experienced a boom in housing development to meet the demand. Another rail track from the quarry ran the length of the shore to Salt Island, so called from the factory opened there in the 18th century to extract salt from sea water. By 1762 this was in ruins but the name still persists. The track was to be the means of carrying stone for the second arm out to sea, but this part of the project was never carried out. Immediately the new harbour was completed it became a refuge for many small boats, as it continues to be today. The quarry area is now a country park, with a visitor centre and exhibition.

The parish church of Holyhead (*Caergybi*) stands above the west side of the inner harbour, as it has done for some seven hundred years. The earliest part of the church is the chancel which formed part of the original building, dedicated to Saint Cybi. Alterations and additions over the years culminated in 1877-9 when the arches from the crossings to the transepts were re-built, the chancel walls received new windows, and in 1896-7 the south chapel was added as a memorial to the philanthropic Stanley family of Penrhos, who were so important to the story of the town. In the church are stained glass windows designed by Edward Burne-Jones and made in the workshop of William Morris.

William Owen Stanley was one of the town's most generous benefactors. He was born in Cheshire, one of twin sons of Sir John Thomas Stanley, the first Lord Stanley of Alderley. He was educated abroad, had travelled widely, but settled at Penrhos on the outskirts of Holyhead (*Caergybi*) after his marriage, and spent the rest of his life serving Anglesey (*Ynys Môn*) in Parliament, furthering his knowledge as an antiquary especially where Anglesey (*Ynys Môn*) was concerned and being particularly generous to Holyhead *(Caergybi)* in his support of local improvements.

He and Elin, his wife, gave £30,000 to local charities during their lifetime, founding the Stanley Hospital and Sailors' Home and providing endowment funds, and they gave £3,000 for the restoration of Saint Cybi's church. The family supplied the town with a piped water system, built the market hall, and contributed to the cost of the new Saint Seiriol's church as the town developed.

This busy man relaxed by painting watercolours, and working in his garden at Penrhos. The house has since been demolished but the present Lord Stanley of Alderley maintains the family interest in Anglesey *(Ynys Môn)* from his home outside Amlwch.

Saint Cybi's church stands within the walls of a Roman fort. The curtain wall, part of which can be seen from the sea, is almost intact. The fort was used as a small coastguard station during the late Roman period. A small building dated early 14th century stands within the churchyard. Called Eglwys y Bedd *(the Church of the Grave)*, as it is reputed to have been built above an ancient grave, it has been used for various purposes including a school set up by Thomas Ellis. His memory is perpetuated in the name given to one of the town's primary schools today.

Thomas Ellis came to Holyhead *(Caergybi)* in 1737 from Jesus College, Oxford, when the lectureship (to say services and to preach) at Saint Cybi's was assigned to him. He later became rector. Thomas Ellis was enthusiastic about education, and began a free school for the poor children of Holyhead *(Caergybi)* for which he unashamedly begged money from every possible source. The school remained at Eglwys y Bedd until 1817 when the National School was built.

Thomas Ellis was fearless in his attempts to clean up the morals of his congregation, and for stressing the sanctity of the Sabbath. He remained in the town until 1759 when he moved to

England.

The fortunes of Holyhead (Caergybi) have fluctuated over the years, the sea having played a large part in its development and its decline. When it became a recognised port for the Irish Sea crossing and mail was shipped to and from Dublin, its future seemed assured. Then followed the harbour development. The inns of the town were kept busy with custom as passengers waited, sometimes for days, for the tides and the weather to allow safe passage. It was when the railway superseded horse-drawn coach travel, and travellers were able to join the ship simply by walking across the station platform from the train, that the town began its slow decline.

Today Holyhead (Caergybi) is regarded as a port of passage by local people, who regret that tourists spend little time in the town itself. The town centre, once a busy marketing and shopping area, is bereft of much of its trade, the current fashion in shopping in the large supermarkets on the outskirts being largely to blame.

In its heyday Holyhead (Caergybi) could boast many characters. As well as the Stanleys and clergy like Thomas Ellis, the town became famous for its almanackers, its sailors and for its lifeboat service. Lifeboat crews around Anglesey (Ynys Môn) are known for their courage and their successes against great odds. Each has its stories to tell. In one hundred and fifty years of service the Holyhead lifeboat saved over thirteen hundred lives.

The old lifeboat station on the Newry beach is now the home of the Holyhead Maritime Museum, where visitors can learn of some of their exploits. And they can also learn the story of the ill-fated Tara, which was the one-time passenger ship Hibernia that made the regular crossing from Holyhead to Ireland. She had been re-named after being requisitioned and made fit for patrol service at the outset of the First World War.

In November, 1915, Tara was sighted in the Mediterranean by a German submarine and torpedoed. Ninety-three of the crew took to the boats, and were towed by the submarine to be landed on the deserted North African coast.

Their horrifying existence for some months, living in the desert under atrocious conditions with very little food, was recorded in the diary of a Holyhead (*Caergybi*) man before they were rescued unexpectedly by a convoy of motor vehicles. The emaciated crew recuperated in an Egyptian hospital before returning, as heroes, to a rapturous welcome at Holyhead (*Caergybi*). The Maritime Museum has pictures of their welcome home.

In 1897 there were no fewer than fifty-eight public houses, inns and hotels in the town, remnants of the days when Holyhead (*Caergybi*) was busy with workers and visitors. Some were of better quality than others. When Dean Swift arrived for his crossing to Ireland in 1727 he was forced to spend several days waiting for fair weather, and his comments on accommodation and hospitality give the impression that there was much to be desired.

Standing on the Alltran Rock at Morawelon, high above the opposite side of the harbour, stands a tall obelisk which travellers approaching the port by sea or by road cannot fail to see.

This was erected to the memory of John Macgregor Skinner, born in America about 1760, the son of the King's Attorney General for New Jersey. He saw many years' service at sea, lost an arm during the American War of Independence, and his right eye in 1780 during wartime service.

Skinner joined the Post Office after his naval service, and in 1799 came to Holyhead (*Caergybi*) in command of a packet boat sailing between Holyhead (*Caergybi*) and Dublin. So began thirty-two years' association with the town. He was outspoken in his criticism of the management of the postal service, complaining that ships were badly constructed and that high fares and poor accommodation for passengers were losing Holyhead (*Caergybi*) valuable trade.

Skinner was returning from Dublin in the packet boat *Escape* on October 30th 1832 when, a short distance from Holyhead (*Caergybi*), a high sea struck the ship and broke into the bulwark where he was standing. He was swept into the sea, and it was some time before his body was washed ashore.

John Macgregor Skinner was so well regarded that his friends erected the memorial to him. The inscription says 'he was distinguished for zeal, intrepidity and fidelity' and records his 'disinterested kindness and unbounded charity'.

Above the town the distinctive tower of Holyhead's (*Caergybi*) one-time convent rises above the rooftops. This building has now been transformed into an eminently successful cultural centre known as Ucheldre, where all kinds of dramatic, artistic and musical events take place.

The end of Telford's London to Holyhead Road was marked by a stone arch of four columns, standing in the harbour. It was built to commemorate the visit of King George IV to Holyhead (*Caergybi*). Thomas Harrison of Chester was the architect. The need for improved road access to the harbour now threatens its existence.

Before the town grew to its present proportions, another skyline feature took the attention of passengers arriving at the port from Ireland. This was the Stanley Mill whose sails caught the Irish Sea winds. It was the last corn mill to work commercially in Wales, when it closed in 1934. The gale force winds of 1938 completed its destruction.

One of the outstanding physical features of Holyhead's (*Caergybi*) skyline today is the tall chimney of the huge aluminium smelter on the outskirts of the town. In the 1960s Holyhead (*Caergybi*) was desperate for new industry which would absorb some of the ever-growing unemployed of this north – west corner of the island and bring some economic stability.

The Rio Tinto Zinc Corporation and Kaiser Aluminium had plans for development. By 1970 their dreams and those of

Holyhead *(Caergybi)* became a merged reality. The smelter plant is huge. The thirty-acre site on which it stands involved the diversion of Telford's Holyhead Road. A new jetty was built in the harbour from where a tunnel under the town carries raw materials to the plant on a conveyor belt. It was a massive project, finished on time. Operating as Anglesey Aluminium Metal Limited, the plant continues to provide employment and gives a boost to the fragile economy of the area.

Holyhead to Llanfair-yng-Nghornwy

The old post road to Holyhead (*Caergybi*) crosses Beddmanarch Bay at its narrowest point, Pont-rhyd-y-bont. When a milestone was erected at Pont-rhyd-y-bont in 1752 it was the fourth from Holyhead (*Caergybi*), hence the English name, Four Mile Bridge. Thomas Telford had plans to carry his road across an embankment from Tŷ Coch, Llanynghenedl, over the bay to Penrhos on Ynys Cybi, so saving five miles (6km) on the journey. Called the Stanley Embankment, in honour of the family over whose land the road passed, it was a major engineering feat and was opened in 1822/3.

The embankment was 1300 yards (1190m) long, and sixteen feet (5m) high above high water. It was set on a sturdy base 114 feet (35m) wide, tapering to 34 feet (10.5m) wide across the top. The rubble for this great dyke was stored in a purposely excavated valley nearby. As soon as 'the Cob' as it was called was opened to traffic, the cluster of dwellings at Tŷ Coch increased in number and the area became known as 'Embankment in the Valley', eventually shortened to 'Valley'.

The embankment was widened during the construction of the Anglesey Aluminium smelter, to carry waterpipes from the Alaw reservoir to the works and electricity cables from Wylfa.

The ordnance survey map shows the long, wide expanse of sand that occupies much of Beddmanarch Bay. Where Afon Alaw flows into the bay are the remains of a large fish weir. Porth Tywyn Mawr and Porth Penrhyn Mawr, deserted in winter, awaken to life with caravans in the summer, and with day visitors who come to enjoy sunshine and sea breezes and watch the Irish ferries moving in and out of Holyhead (*Caergybi*). From Porth Tywyn Mawr the coastline is more dramatic, and wide, sandy bays are fewer.

The remains of a windmill high above Porth Swtan (*Church Bay*) remind one of the days when Anglesey (*Ynys Môn*) boasted many such mills. The early post mills were of timber, but none remain. Travelling around Anglesey *(Ynys Môn)* one sees many ruined stone towers of 18th and 19th century mills, their caps and sails long since gone. Some have been converted into unique houses or office accommodation.

The 1851 census records over one hundred corn mills on the island during that year. Most of these fell into disuse between 1856 and 1900. They could not compete with the steamdriven mills introduced to the cities by the industrial revolution, and many Anglesey *(Ynys Môn)* housewives began to buy flour milled in Liverpool as it was cheaper. Millers started to crush food for cattle, but farmers began to do this for themselves as they could buy their own crushers. When mill machinery broke down it was not mended or replaced. Ruined mill towers without their caps are a feature of the Anglesey *(Ynys Môn)* landscape today.

What is reputed to be the last thatched cottage in Anglesey *(Ynys Môn)* stands near the shore at Porth Swtan. Owned by the National Trust, this has now been leased to a conservation group, the Friends of Swtan, and has been fully restored. The work has involved re-roofing with willow laths and wheat straw laid on gorse, the re-building of a *crog-lofft* (roof space) and cowshed, removing a considerable amount of debris from the cottage floor and fitting an old grate to bring the cottage back to the state in which it would have appeared early in the 19th century.

Swtan was first mentioned in Leyland's *Itinerary* of 1536/39, and is legally documented from 1678. The cottage is now open to visitors on certain days during the summer.

'Swtan' is Welsh for whiting. Because the spire of Llanrhuddland Church was so prominent from the sea, a marine chart of 1816 called Porth Swtan 'Church Bay', a name since adopted by monoglot English speakers.

At Carmel Head, which is the north-western tip of Anglesey *(Ynys Môn)*, at Penbryn yr Eglwys, there is slight evidence of a small church founded in the 6th or 7th centuries, another instance of an early church or cell built on a remote site by a religious recluse seeking peace to worship. Later, possibly in the 10th century, because of its suitability as a look-out site, Carmel Head may have been a cliff fort.

Ynys y Fydlyn is at the end of a steep valley down which once ran a series of telegraph poles and wires linking the Skerries with mainland Anglesey *(Ynys Môn)*. It is claimed that Vikings made a landing here.

The Skerries (Ynysoedd y Moelrhoniaid – Islands of the Seals) is a cluster of rocks. On one stands a lighthouse, important to shipping rounding the treacherous north coast of Ynys Môn to enter Liverpool Bay. This area of turbulent seas has seen many shipwrecks and brave rescue attempts.

In November 1890 the Swedish ship *Hudiksvall*, a sailing ship, barque-rigged, was making her way from Liverpool to New York in ballast when she was forced towards Holyhead *(Caergybi)* to shelter from strong winds. But her anchor did not hold. She was driven north towards Carmel Head and sent urgent distress signals. Holyhead lifeboat put to sea in response, but when she reached the *Hudiksvall* found the ship on her beam ends with two broken masts. The crew were hanging on. The lifeboat threw a rope which the crew secured and sixteen were able to scramble to safety as their ship broke up and sank.

In 1881 the sailing vessel *Gilbert Thompson*, nineteen years old and iron-built, was under tow with a tug on the last part of her journey from Calcutta to Liverpool. As the ships were negotiating the channel between the Skerries and the West Mouse, the *Gilbert Thompson* keeled over with the strong tide and the iron hull was torn savagely on jagged underwater rocks. The crew of twenty-two, except for a cabin boy with a broken leg, managed to scramble to safety on to the rocks before the vessel sank. The men were rescued by the tug and taken to Liverpool.

But perhaps the most famous wreck of all was that of the

Mary, the first royal yacht. When Charles, Pretender to the English throne, was banished to the continent he spent time in Holland where his sister Mary had married the Prince of Orange.

On Charles's accession, William presented him with a luxurious Dutch yacht which was named *Mary*. She was a large ship, manned by a crew of thirty, but her life as a royal yacht was short because she was unsuited to sailing conditions in the Thames. So she was put into service to carry important passengers between England and Ireland.

In March 1675 *Mary* was wrecked close to the Skerries. As she capsized, her long mainmast touched the shore and thirty-nine passengers and crew were able to reach safety. The captain, bo'sun and thirty-four other passengers perished. It was some time before the passengers were taken off the island. In those days there was no light on the Skerries, and the north-west coast of Môn was sparsely populated.

A chance dive by Lancashire sub aqua clubs in 1971 located two of *Mary's* bronze guns. Marine researchers were alerted. Nine bronze guns and other artefacts were eventually brought up from the sea bed. Now the Maritime Museum at Liverpool cares for nearly 1500 objects from the wreck including guns, an anchor, silver coins, fine table ware and jewellery, even a skeleton of a woman passenger.

The rocks on which the Skerries lighthouse stands are at the end of a strip of submerged land which lies directly in the path of the major shipping lines from Liverpool to Ireland.

A light was proposed on the Skerries by a private speculator who saw lucrative possibilities from the tolls that could be levied, but it was not until 1714 that the then leaseholder, William Trench, was given permission to erect a light. For a Crown rent of £5 a year he was given the right to levy dues of one penny per ship and twopence per ton of cargo. But it was not to be the profitable venture he envisaged, however. When the coalfire light in a basket was first kindled in 1714, Trench was a wealthy man, but traders and mariners evading payment sent him into debt and when he died in 1729 he was ruined. After William Trench's death the lease passed to his daughter and an Act of Parliament was passed giving her and her family the sole claim to the Skerries.

In 1834, when Trinity House tried to buy the patent, the then owner refused, saying that he had no responsibility to sell. By this time the Skerries had become a profitable investment. Finally it was bought by Trinity House in 1841, for the vast sum of £444,984, the last privately owned lighthouse in the British Isles to be acquired by them.

Trench's light was a round tower about 35 feet (11m) tall with an open bucket-shaped grate on top that consumed eighty to one hundred tons of coal each year. In 1804/5 a new lighthouse was built, with an oil-lit lantern and reflectors. It was converted to electricity in 1927, and subsequently in 1987 to automatic operation, and de-manned. It is now monitored and controlled remotely from the Trinity House Operations Control Centre at Harwich.

Tradition has it that the consequences of a certain shipwreck off this coast in the late 18th century were to have far-reaching effects on the development of orthopaedic surgery in Britain in later years. A smuggler put out to sea on a stormy night and came across a sinking vessel with two boys clinging to it. He took them aboard. One child died, but he was able to reach land safely with the other and took him to Mynachdy, the house of a Dr Lloyd, who gave the boy a home. The boy's first name was Evan, and he was given the surname Thomas. Evan was believed to be a Spaniard and had no English or Welsh.

Evan Thomas possessed an inherent art of bonesetting. This first showed when he mended the broken leg of a chicken. His ability impressed Dr Lloyd who took him on his rounds and the boy was given every encouragement to use his talent until his name became a byword in Anglesey (Ynys Môn) and beyond. A generation after Evan Thomas's death there were twenty one members of the family who were doctors or recognised bonesetters.

Evan Thomas's grandson, another Evan, set up in practice in Liverpool. He had seven children. One, Hugh Owen Thomas, was trained as a doctor. He worked with his father but later had his own surgery in Liverpool where he devised surgical instruments, made his own splints, and designed plasters and bandages. His teaching methods were way ahead of his time, and today the site at 11 Nelson Street, Liverpool is remembered as the birthplace of modern orthopaedic surgery. His name still lives in 'the Thomas splint'. Evan Thomas's nephew was Sir Robert Jones whose name will always be associated with the famous orthopaedic hospital at Gobowen.

Mynachdy, which was home to young Evan Thomas, stands remote between the village of Llanfair-yng-Nghornwy and the rocky shore at Hen Borth. It was built in the late 17th century and, in its early days, belonged to the Cistercian Abbey of Aberconwy although there is no evidence that monks ever occupied it. In the cellar is a walled-in doorway that opened to a tunnel leading to the shore.

The quiet little village of Llanfair-yng-Nghornwy has a singular connection with the sea. To the rectory in the early 19th century came Frances as the young bride of the rector, James Williams. Her husband was a keen supporter of the Association for the Preservation of Life from Shipwreck, and Frances encouraged his interest.

In 1823 the sailing packet *Alert*, travelling from Howth to Parkgate, was becalmed off the northern Anglesey (*Ynys Môn*) coast and driven by a strong tide on to the rocks at West Mouse (*Maen y Bugail*). The ship sank soon after being holed, and only seven of the one hundred and forty-seven passengers and crew managed to scramble into a small boat and were rescued. Twenty-seven bodies were recovered and buried at Holyhead (*Caergybi*). The remainder were never found.

James and Frances Williams watched in horror, helpless,

from the shore, and decided that never again should such a tragedy happen without there being assistance available. So they persuaded the newly-formed National Lifeboat Institution to provide a boat to be stationed at Cemlyn, opposite the sunken rocks known as Harry Furlong's.

Frances and James Williams founded the Anglesey *(Ynys Môn)* branch of the Royal National Lifeboat Institution for the Preservation of Life from Shipwreck and worked tirelessly for it. James not only initiated activity in this way, but also gave brave physical assistance during rescue attempts.

During the years 1828 to 1856 over four hundred lives were saved by lifeboats off the coast of Anglesey *(Ynys Môn)*.

Llanfair-yng-Nghornwy to Wylfa

Harry Furlong's Rocks mark the opening to Cemlyn Bay, the haunt of sea birds who congregate in their thousands seeking the quieter waters of the lagoon beyond the spit – and the haunt of ornithologists who congregate to see them.

The house almost hidden behind a high wall is Bryn Aber, one-time home of Vivian Hewitt, dubbed the 'modest millionaire' by his biographer, William Hywel who was his doctor for many years and knew him well.

In his biography, Dr Hywel recounts Hewitt's amazing life. He was an exceptionally wealthy man whose fortune came from the family brewing industry in Grimsby. His branch of that family lived at Bodfari in Denbighshire. Vivian's father insisted that his son should prove himself able to earn his own living and so, in the early 1900s, he chose to study engineering and worked in the marine engineering department at Portsmouth dockyard, occupied in building in first Dreadnought.

Steam engines proved an early passion, and he went to Crewe railway sheds as an apprentice in 1905. During four years there he gained a wide experience of working in a signal box, rail track laying, and as an auxiliary fireman on the footplate of expresses running from Crewe to Holyhead (*Caergybi*).

Having proved his ability, Hewitt was given a generous family allowance, and returned home to a life of comparative luxury, to spend his time experimenting with gliders, powered aircraft, motor cycles and cars.

Vivian Hewitt engaged two assistants, and hired a shed on the motor racing circuit at Brooklands where they dealt in second hand cars and repairs. The developing aircraft industry proved a fascination. A doting uncle gave Vivian Hewitt an aeroplane, and he was to buy two more himself over the next few years.

In 1912 Vivian Hewitt flew from Rhyl, where he had bought a field, the seventy-five miles (120km) to Dublin via Holyhead (*Caergybi*), so creating the world's record in aviation over water. By this time he had moved into lodgings in Rhyl, where his landlady and her family were to be his housekeeper and house servants and companions in the future, moving with him wherever he chose to live.

Most of Hewitt's war years were spent in America where he tested aircraft engines. While there, he had an accident. His injuries and a heart condition precluded any further flying adventures and he switched his attention to motor boats. He returned to Rhyl for the next ten years.

An interest in ornithology involved the use of a motor boat. His trips took him and his companions to South Wales and the Llŷn peninsular where he would rent houses near to an area noted for birds, taking with him his housekeeper. His favourite area was Anglesey (*Ynys Môn*). One year he rented Ynys Seiriol (*Puffin Island*) from the Baron Hill estate, where he studied puffins and many other sea birds, living in one of the coastguard cottages on the shore at Penmon.

His bird-watching took him around the coast of Anglesey (*Ynys Môn*). He found Cemlyn, leased Bryn Aber, and gradually bought land around with the aim of creating a bird sanctuary which eventually was to cover 272 acres. To improve conditions for the birds, he built a dam which had the effect of increasing the depth of water.

As farms became vacant, Hewitt bought them, demolished the buildings and was planning to plant a forest until the Second World War put paid to his plans as the land was earmarked for agriculture.

He built the massive wall surrounding Bryn Aber with the intention of making the garden a bird sanctuary as the wall would protect trees and shrubs from salt spray and east winds. Rats would be kept out as the wall was set directly on to rock and topped with scale-proof smooth stone. There was no door in Hewitt's day. The eccentric owner and his staff and visitors had to climb ladders to enter the property. And he built a cavity wall, with observation windows on the inner skin so that bird-watchers using the passage in between could see the birds without being observed.

As Britain's tax system demanded higher taxes from the wealthy, Vivian Hewitt went to live in the Bahamas, but retained Bryn Aber where he kept his comprehensive collection of birds' eggs. After his death, four furniture vans were needed to move the collection to the British Trust for Ornithology's premises in Tring.

In Vivian Hewitt's day, Bryn Aber had no water or electricity. In spite of his vast wealth, which could have been the means of providing such amenities on a site as remote as Cemlyn, this odd character scorned the basic home comforts. Yet, when he needed to visit London, he would travel first class and stay at the Savoy Hotel.

Vivian Hewitt returned to Anglesey *(Ynys Môn)* a sick man, and died here in 1965. Visitors to Bryn Aber today no longer need to scale a wall to enter. The sheltered wall garden is a garden of remembrance to the man whose ashes are buried beneath one of the trees he planted. The Cemlyn Nature Reserve is now in the capable hands of the North Wales Wildlife Trust.

A wide variety of birds, including gulls, terns, plovers, oystercatchers, redshanks and several species of water fowl are seen here in their seasons. As well as being a wonderland for bird watchers, Cemlyn's storm beach and shingle bar is the home of many common plants found in such a habitat – sea beet, thrift, sea campion, crisped dock and an extensive growth of sea kale.

In between Cemlyn Bay and the gaunt skyline of the Wylfa Power Station lies the small bay of Porth y Pistyll, with the old water mill of Melin Cafnan on the shore, and behind it the secret and very lovely garden of Cestyll.

The garden was once a part of Cestyll house, since demolished, when it was owned by the Hon. Violet Vivian who was a courtier at the time of Queen Alexandra. Violet Vivian used Cestyll as a summer residence, and developed the idyllic rocky garden, retaining its natural setting. The garden passed into other hands in 1961, and has been owned and maintained by Wylfa Power Station since 1983. The Power Station has continued Violet Vivian's tradition of opening the garden to the public since 1985, although this is restricted to one day a year in May, with proceeds of admission going to charity.

Melin Cafnan and its machinery, dating from 1840, now belong to the National Trust who have no plans for public access. There is evidence to suggest that a water mill has been operating on this site since the 13th century. The mill is unusual in that the race water flows over the top of the mill wheel when in operation, and is diverted under the wheel when not required.

Construction of the Wylfa Magnox Power Station began in 1963 and reactor 1 started generating in January 1971. As was to be expected, there was opposition locally, some still evident today which surfaces as soon as there is any stoppage due to parts failure.

Reactor 2 began generating in June 1971. During construction, the labour force was estimated to be between two thousand and three thousand. There is a permanent staff complement of around six hundred. Magnox Electric PLC merged with British Nuclear Fuels Ltd in 1998.

On a typical day, Wylfa will supply 23mKWH of electricity, enough to meet the needs of two cities the size of Liverpool.

Wylfa to Amlwch

Cemaes Bay is a hive of activity in the summer when visitors arrive, and it would appear that tourism is its only industry. But it has not always been so, for during the early 19th century it was one of the busiest small ports in Anglesey *(Ynys Môn)* throughout the year.

Before the improvement in overland travel, it was easier to bring goods in to Anglesey *(Ynys Môn)* by sea, and although the original harbour at Cemaes was nothing more than a landing place, every use was made of it. Small boats would seek shelter in the bay during a storm. Herring fishing was at its height, and fishermen landed their catches to be salted. Ships delivered coal, and filled their empty holds with limestone, bricks, lime and paint. Limestone from Porth Padrig was loaded here for Liverpool, to be used in city centre public buildings. The copper industry at nearby Mynydd Parys also contributed to the port's trade, and, between 1801 and 1831, its growing success boosted the population figure by four hundred for the parish of Llanbadrig, to which Cemaes belonged.

It was evident that if Cemaes Bay was to take advantage of its trading possibilities, something would have to be done about providing a pier. Ishmael Jones was a local sea captain and entrepreneur, and it was he who built Cemaes Bay's first pier. He began to build ships, too, his boatyard employing sixty men. A violent storm in 1889 destroyed most of Ishmael Jones's pier. It was rebuilt and extended in 1900 at a cost of over £1500.

Trade at the port declined when the copper industry failed, and when the railway to Holyhead *(Caergybi)* and Amlwch was opened.

In the early days, the village was called Castell Iorwerth, after Prince Iorwerth who held court here. Later it became known as Cemais, the name of the hundred in which it was sited, and was re-named Cemaes Bay in 1911 to distinguish it from Cemaes, in mid Wales.

Many visitors to Cemaes Bay make the pilgrimage to the tiny parish church of Llanbadrig on the cliff to the east of the bay. This is one of the oldest ecclesiastical sites in Wales, where the dedication to Saint Patrick is unique in that it has direct reference to the saint who is said to have founded a cell here. The story goes that Patrick, on his way to Ireland, was shipwrecked off shore and in gratitude for making land safely founded his cell on this spot. This happened around A.D.440, but the church of today dates from the 14th century.

The building was restored in 1884, endowed by Lord Stanley of Alderley, although he was a Moslem, which explains the Islamic influence in the interior of the church – the blue, red and white stained glass, and the blue tiles around the altar.

Vandals set fire to Llanbadrig church in 1985 and after a great money-raising effort on the part of parishioners and sympathisers it was restored at a cost of £15,000, only to be fired again just as it was to be re-consecrated. The parishioners made another effort to raise funds (this time the cost was £30,000), again successfully.

The small humped island off the coast between Llanbadrig and Porth Llanlleiana, West Mouse or Ynys Badrig, has another intriguing Welsh name – Maen y Bugail (*the Shepherd's Stone*), which invites a story. Folk lore tells that an old shepherd looking after his sheep on the cliffs above the sea was irritated by a stone in his shoe. Angrily he shook it out and tossed it into the sea, whereupon the island arose, magically, out of the waves.

Opposite Ynys Badrig is Porth Llanlleiana, above which are the remains of yet another early church and, close to the shore, the ruins of a china clay works. Porth Llanlleiana is sheltered to the north-east by a headland, the site of the ancient fort of Dinas Gynfor. This was a large fort, strategically placed as it was bounded on three sides by precipitous cliffs to the sea, and on the fourth side by a steep slope leading down to a marshy valley, the ideal site from which to repel raiders from the sea.

The tower was erected to commemorate the accession of King Edward VII.

Down below the rocks of Porth Wen are the remains of a brickworks which was active during the early years of the century up to the First World War, producing high quality bricks of a yellow-white colour which were valued for their special quality of being able to withstand very high temperatures because of the high percentage of silica contained in the clay.

In 1906 a German became the owner. He specialised in making bricks by the wire-cutting method. Two years later he was followed by Charles Tidy who was to remain in charge until the works closed in 1914. Tidy expanded the scope of the works, and introduced the press technique, producing glazed bricks and tiles.

It is hard to imagine an industry on a more difficult site. Problems in transport were to be among the factors contributing to the closure of the Porth Wen brickworks. Road transport was out of the question. A quay did exist, but the sea at Porth Wen often carried a heavy swell, and ship owners were loth to allow their vessels to stay at the quayside as they were likely to be damaged by striking the rocky bed.

As a dramatic background to this part of the coastline, a modern wind farm soars above the skyline. This is Rhyd-y-groes, its twenty-four wind turbines whose blades began turning in 1992 produce around 20,000 MW of electricity for the National Grid every year.

East of Porth Wen the sea scours the wide scoop of Bull Bay, past the small indentation of Porth Llechog. This area was noted for its fishing and smuggling, two occupations which often appeared together.

As well as being a lifeboat station, Porth Llechog was also a pilot station in the days when shipping lines operated their own piloting services through a number of stations along the coast. Two four-oared sailing pilot boats were moored here. In the early 19th century, like many of the bays along the Anglesey (*Ynys Môn*) coast, Porth Llechog had its own small ship yard.

The name, Bull Bay, comes from the deep pool on the shore called in Welsh, Pwll y Tarw.

This coastline was a favourite haunt of the 3rd Marquess of Anglesey, who intended to build another home here. In 1864 he commissioned Evan Pritchard to create a swimming bath which was completed, but the house was never built. The designer's flight of fancy for the swimming bath created a medieval gateway flanked by round towers, complete with guard rooms. The entrance opened to a walled court with flower beds. There were stone dressing rooms from which a sloping pathway led down to the bath, cut out of the rock, twenty yards long by ten feet wide. The bath was cleaned and refilled by each tide. Called The Roman Bath by the local people, it has since deteriorated. The building is a ruin and only the cavity in the rock remains.

Looking at Amlwch today one has little conception of the changes that have taken place there since the middle of the 18th century. In those days it was merely a hamlet, but when copper was found in Mynydd Parys to the south, and mined, it became a flourishing town. As Bingley, the contemporary traveller through Wales, commented, Amlwch was 'entirely dependent for its prosperity on the copper mines, for most of its inhabitants have some concern in them, either as miners or agents'. Suddenly, it became a prosperous market town with shops and its own brewery and some small industries.

Aikin, writing in 1797, said 'The town of Amlwch which about thirty years ago had no more than half a dozen houses in the whole parish now supports a population of four or five thousand'.

This rapid growth brought its problems. James Treweek, the Cornish mine agent whose family was to play a large part in the industrial history of the town, stated 'Amlwch is one of the worst places I ever knew for young men to be brought up in

. . . because of the many pot houses in the town and the company who attend them regularly'.

In the Mona Mine Mss there is a comment on the town's medical profession . . . 'There are three doctors at Amlwch. One is a drunkard, the second lacks experience and surgical skill and the third is habitually in the same condition as the first'. Those comments can be understood when one remembers that at the time of their writing there were no less than sixty public houses in Amlwch.

Two men stand out in the industrial story of Amlwch – Thomas Williams and James Treweek.

Thomas Williams was an Anglesey *(Ynys Môn)* lawyer who became one of the most important figures in the Industrial Revolution in Britain. His connection with Amlwch began when he was called in by the Lewis family of Llys Dulas to sort out their boundary claim to part of Mynydd Parys when a vein of copper was discovered there. He became involved in the business and joined with two others to create the Parys Mine Company which was eventually to employ eight hundred workers. He then formed a second, the Mona Mine Company, which gave him control of mining the other side of the mountain.

These two companies were to become one of the greatest industrial projects of the 18th century and made Thomas Williams a wealthy man. He built smelting works at Amlwch, Ravenhead and Swansea and brass and copper works at Holywell, in South Wales and the Thames Valley; there were offices and stores at Liverpool, and he diversified with commercial ventures in Chester, Bangor and Caernarfon. He also took over the Cornish copper industry. By 1800 it was claimed that half the copper market, worth around one million pounds, was in the hands of Thomas Williams.

First and foremost, he was an Ynys Môn Welshman, quick to contribute to the new church at Amlwch in 1800, and farming his lands wisely. Always quick to attach a sobriquet, Anglesey *(Ynys Môn)* men called Thomas Williams 'Twm Chwarae Teg'

(Tom Fair Play), which reflected his attitude to his fellow men in all walks of life.

Treweek's association with Amlwch came through the Cornish copper industry. He came to Amlwch from Cornwall in 1811, as manager to the new Mona Mine Company. His responsibilities were varied. He superintended all the mining operations and had a staff of several hundred. He organised transport of goods to and from the mine, using local farmers with their carts. He had the power to grant or refuse work, never a popular situation for a manager. He fixed rates of pay for piece work, dealt with strikes, and saw to medical services at the mine where accidents were frequent.

After 1833 until his death in 1851 he was in charge of everything connected with copper mining and the Amlwch copper trade, and it is thanks to his ability in all these fields that the copper industry in Amlwch flourished as it did.

The sudden influx of workers to Amlwch found the parish church inadequate to meet their needs. Church records show that in 1792 it was felt necessary to put up a new building. The mine companies offered a contribution of £600 towards the cost, provided the remainder was met through local rates. But the Bishop of Bangor disagreed, saying the companies should meet the whole cost themselves.

On the death of the Bishop, the problems were solved, and the new Bishop consecrated the new church in 1800. Amlwch was proud of its new edifice, which had an organ and a choir gallery. The final cost was £2,500 to which the mine owners, the Earl of Uxbridge, the Revd Edward Hughes and Thomas Williams contributed.

During the last part of the 18th century, before copper was discovered in Mynydd Parys, the port at Amlwch was little more than a deep water creek where fishing boats could shelter from a storm. The Parys Mining Company built a small pier in 1782 when it realised that better facilities would be needed to handle cargoes, and in 1793 an Act was passed 'to enlarge, deepen, cleanse and improve' the harbour which allowed shelter for thirty sloops from sixty to one hundred tons.

In 1827 storm force winds drove the sea up to the neck of the harbour, and a barrier of movable wooden baulks was built which could be set in position to act as a breakwater. Rules regarding entering and leaving the port were then strictly enforced, which involved crews of visiting ships manhandling the baulks, a practice unpopular with them from its inception.

Shipbuilding was an important new industry in Amlwch in the 1820s when The Anglesey Shipping Company was formed. James Treweek's sons built small cutters and larger vessels of up to about two hundred tons at Amlwch Port, and repair work was carried out. By the middle of the 19th century they had ceased their association but despite the decline of the copper trade the shipbuilding industry continued for a while longer. The last ship to be built at Amlwch was launched in 1912.

In 1851 James Treweek died and the copper industry in Anglesey (Ynys Môn) started to fall into decline. The opening of the railway line to Amlwch proved the death knell to the port, as freight charges by rail were cheaper than those by sea.

With the demise of the Parys Mountain copper mining industry, unemployment followed and Amlwch went further into decline. The harbour buildings fell into disuse, and it is only in recent years that conservation and regeneration has re-created interest in the past.

Amlwch's chief industry today is that of the Octel plant where bromine is extracted from sea water. The works are on the shore close to the harbour.

During the latter decades of the twentieth century the north coast of Anglesey (Ynys Môn) boasted an offshore oil terminal. Pipes were laid across the island and oil was pumped ashore, through these and under the Menai Strait and along the coast to oil storage terminals at Stanlow in Cheshire. Shell Oil, whose project it was, contributed generously to the island in several ways, and although the project was comparatively short-lived there are still communities benefiting from the funds they provided.

There is an ever-present reminder of copper in Amlwch today. The road from the town to Llannerch-y-medd climbs Mynydd Parys and passes the western side of the old workings, revealing the 'lunar landscape' dereliction where many of those workings were abandoned in the mid-19th century. There have been researches in recent years to discover whether or not re-opening to abstract other minerals might be viable, but market conditions have been unfavourable.

Today, it is left to local historians to guide visitors over the mountain in the summer to tell its story.

Amlwch to Dulas

It is only a short distance from Amlwch to Point Lynas, yet at this north-eastern extremity of Anglesey *(Ynys Môn)* one might be in another world. Gone are the signs of active and defunct industry. Instead, the rocky coastline is backed by gentle green fields, with the unique tower of Llaneilian church above the tiny bay of Porth yr Ychen and, around the bluff, the more incised bay of Porth Eilian overlooked by the lighthouse at Point Lynas.

Llaneilian parish church is ancient. The tower, a stocky, square edifice crowned with a simple stone spire, was built around eight hundred years ago. The chancel and the nave were rebuilt in the 15th century. The chapel of Saint Eilian, at an angle to the chancel and connected to it by a 17th century passage, dates from the late 14th or early 15th century and was built on the site of Saint Eilian's cell which was a place of worship in the year 500.

Saint Eilian was a sixth century saint who, with his family and possessions, sailed from Rome and landed at Porth yr Ychain. Eilian is said to have restored the sight of Prince Caswallon who, in thanks, gave him land on which to settle. Eilian's well, Ffynnon Eilian on the coast, now in ruins, was reputed for its curative powers. Eilian built his cell near to the landing place, and the present church is said to have been built over the site of his shrine.

The church has some interesting antiquities in its decor and furnishings. Wood carvings include angels playing musical instruments. The rood screen carries a painting of the grim reaper, a salutary reminder to every worshipper.

In a time when local saints' days provided an excuse for celebration in the form of recreation, *Gwyliau Mabsant* as these days were called, were often held on Sundays. They were popular celebrations when no holds were barred until reforms were introduced. One of the most popular of these celebrations to which revellers from all over Anglesey *(Ynys Môn)* came was that at Llaneilian, held on the first three Fridays in August.

Here pedlars sold their wares, excessive drinking led to all kinds of social misdemeanours, games were played and there was wanton behaviour. Each parish had its own individual attractions. People flocking to Llaneilian would attempt to lie in Eilian's chest, a church chest measuring four feet square by three feet deep. Anyone who could turn around in the confined space would have his or her life extended for another year, or so it was believed. A narrow division in a wooden panel in the church presented a challenge to young people to pass through it without touching the sides, for good luck. But failure reversed the good fortune.

These were times when superstition was rife, and it took the Roundheads and, later, the Nonconformists especially, to stamp out many of the old traditions.

As in every coastal churchyard in Anglesey *(Ynys Môn)*, where there are memorials to sea captains or sailors, Llaneilian has its share. Some of those seamen left evidence of their experiences through the letters they wrote home to their families. John Roberts of Llaneilian, a second mate on a tall ship built at Amlwch, was one such. He sailed to the far east and South America. He was presumed dead in 1882, at only twenty-four years of age, when his ship failed to reach port.

As the port of Liverpool was expanding, the need was felt in 1766 for a station on Anglesey *(Ynys Môn)* from where ships could pick up a pilot to take them safely in and out of the Mersey. Before this time, pilotage was privately operated, with no supervision. In 1764 eighteen ships had been stranded and more than seventy-five lives lost. Traffic in and out of the river was increasing rapidly. That same year, seventy-four vessels left the Mersey for Africa, the slave trade being in full swing, and a hundred and forty-one ships sailed for America. Liverpool had become the second busiest port in the United Kingdom.

In 1766 the first Liverpool Pilotage Act was passed and its rules were stringent. By 1771 by-laws allowed for four sloops between Point Lynas and Ynys Seiriol *(Puffin Island)*. These were forty-ton vessels with 'two lanthorns, one swivel gun and a good spying glass; they must carry six or seven pilots and two or three apprentices each'.

'Every boat must wear a broad vane with her number on it; her name, Master's name and number painted on both sides of all her sails, four feet in length near the head, with black, in fair characters which must be renewed twice a year. Each boat shall have two masters who must go out by turns and carry their full complement of pilots with them.'

All the ships approaching Point Lynas had to hoist their colours and show lights or fire guns by night and run close inshore so they could be boarded in smooth water.

By 1896, steam had taken over and two ships were based at Point Lynas. Forty-three pilots were attached, including two masters. Thirteen pilots remained ashore for harbour duty. Later motor vessels were used.

At first the early pilots used a farmhouse as their lookout post. From 1799 they used two oil lamps with small metal reflectors set into a tower and showing in two directions, and there was a flagstaff for day signals. A lighthouse was built in 1835 by the Mersey Docks and Harbour Board at a cost of £1,165. The lighthouse is a low, castellated building painted white with round lens rooms connected to the seaward side of the house.

Trinity House assumed responsibility for the Point Lynas lighthouse in 1973. It was electrified in 1951 and automated in 1989. There is an automatic fog detector which activates the fog signal should visibility drop to less than two and a half miles (4km). The old pilot house no longer exists.

Robert Beaver, an Anglesey *(Ynys Môn)* sailor and trader, was at one time responsible for the lighthouse and pilot station on a voluntary basis, although he did benefit from the occasional cask of wine which might have slipped the notice of the customs at Holyhead *(Caergybi)*. And he had useful deliveries of coal and cloth. He later appealed to Liverpool Corporation for a yearly allowance which was granted.

Beaver, born in Aberffraw in 1748, had an adventurous life. He went to sea at an early age and soon commanded his own ship. He traded linens and woollens and other commodities with the west coast of Africa where he picked up slaves for the colonies and West Indies, trading them there for cotton and sugar to bring back to Britain.

By 1781 he had received his Letter of Marque, the commission authorising a privateer to make reprisals on a hostile nation until satisfaction for injury had been duly made. He owned and commanded the largest privateer in the West Indies, with which he had a long run of success. In less than three years Beaver had captured over fifty prizes, made his name as a daring and successful commander, and amassed a fortune. Ill health forced him to leave the sea, and he returned home in 1782, after which he settled with his wife and eleven children at Maes y Llwyn, Amlwch and took responsibility for the Point Lynas light. He died there about 1812.

The telecommunications masts on Mynydd Eilian are a reminder of the earlier method of sending messages, when a semaphore station stood on the high land above Point Lynas. This was the third station in line from South Stack on Ynys Cybi *(Holy Island)*, signalling messages to a similar station on Ynys Seiriol to be relayed several more times along the coast before arriving at Liverpool.

Beyond the radio masts, at the entrance to Dulas Bay, is the estate of Llysdulas which looks out to Ynys Dulas with its tower standing on the rock. The old parish church of Saint Gwenllwyfo, now nothing more than a ruin, stood on the estate. The present church dates from 1856.

When William Lewis Hughes who had inherited Llysdulas retired from Parliament, where he had served as Member for

Wallingford, he was created Lord Dinorben and looked forward to living permanently in Anglesey (Ynys Môn), improving his estate and building a new church. But he died before this could be done. In the event, his wife carried out his wishes and donated nearly one thousand pounds towards the cost, a princely sum in those days.

One might be forgiven for wondering why such a large church was thought necessary in this sparsely populated area, but the Dinorben family enjoyed entertaining and some of the parties were large, bringing with them an army of servants. And everyone attended church from Llysdulas.

Lady Dinorben's daughter married into the Neave family. Sir Thomas Neave had been a collector of art works and antiques, including stained glass from the continent. Some of this was donated by his grandson to Llanwenllwyfo church in 1877, and mounted inside the existing glass windows.

In his booklet describing the glass, Rector's Warden J.O. Hughes quotes the curator of the Metropolitan Museum of Art in New York 'The two best places in the world to see Neave Flemish glass is the Metropolitan Museum of Art in New York and Llanwenllwyfo Church in Europe'.

Many of the panels in Llanwenllwyfo came from a Carthusian monastery in Louvain in Belgium. The glass is picturesque and gently colourful. It must have been a source of interest and inspiration during long Victorian sermons.

One panel depicting the scene after the resurrection in the Garden shows Jesus wearing a straw hat. The priests of the Vatican in the early 16th century felt that for the picture to be acceptable to simple people Jesus needed to be depicted as the gardener wearing a hat. This glass was made in Malines in about 1522.

The tower standing on Ynys Dulas was erected by Lady Dorina Neave, as she was touched by the plight of the crews of small ships wrecked in storms off the coast at Dulas. She provided a fireplace as part of the tower, with kindling. There was a flask of brandy, drinking water and biscuits, as refreshment for shipwrecked sailors. But the passing of sail saw the end of most of the shipwrecks. The last use made of Ynys Dulas was by three airmen whose aircraft had come down in the sea and they rowed to the rock in a dinghy, to find the tower devoid of fuel or food.

Traeth Dulas, a wide stretch of sand and mud flats when the tide is out, is almost encircled by land and, in the days of small coastal vessels, provided a natural harbour. The land running down to the shore on the south side was farmed from the old house of Pentre Erianell which was the home of a very remarkable family who contributed a great deal to the story of Anglesey (*Ynys Môn*).

Dulas to Moelfre

Ynys Môn has six 'mountains', although their height (none over 220 metres) suggests that this is a misnomer. Mynydd Twr *(Holyhead Mountain)* (220m) and Mynydd Parys (147m) have already been seen on the journey around the coast. The village of Llanfair-yng-Nghornwy lies at the foot of Mynydd y Garn (170m); Mynydd Eilian (177m) to the south of Point Lynas is made more conspicuous by the group of telecommunications masts on its eastern flank. Mynydd Bodafon (178m) is the high land seen from Dulas, and Mynydd Llwydiarth (158m) overlooks Pentraeth and Traeth Coch.

The narrow road from Brynrefail, between Dulas and Lligwy, climbs the broad breast of Mynydd Bodafon, skirting the summit to pass through a col where cottages stand on the edge of a tarn, before dropping down steeply to Maenaddwyn and the centre of Anglesey *(Ynys Môn)*. This tarn is a magical place, reed-fringed and peaceful with a tangible atmosphere. The rocks forming Mynydd Bodafon are quartzite, the oldest in Wales. In the rough heathland are the remains of ancient hut circles and a medieval homestead.

By the side of the main road linking Dinas Dulas and Brynrefail stands a stone column commemorating the Morris brothers whose home was at Pentre Erianell nearby, the farm whose lands sloped down to Bae Dulas.

The four brothers, Lewis, William, Richard and John, each talented in their individual ways, were obsessional letter writers. Their importance to our understanding of life in Wales in the 18th century arises through the content of those letters, as they wrote to each other as freely as they would have spoken together.

The least well known of the brothers was John, who went to sea at an early age and lost his life in naval action off the coast of Spain when he was thirty-four years old. Richard left Ynys Môn to seek his fortune in London. After months of near penury he obtained a post at the Admiralty where he rose eventually to be chief clerk for foreign accounts to the Comptroller of the Navy, a responsible position.

Richard Morris's main claim to fame was as founder of the Cymmrodorion Society based in London, a society which remains in existence to this day, noted for its scholarly lectures on Welsh matters, and for its Transactions.

The brothers wrote no fewer than one thousand letters to each other, and four hundred of those were written by the second brother, William, to Richard. William spent most of his life in Holyhead *(Caergybi)*, where he was comptroller of customs. Like his brothers, he was an avid reader and collected manuscripts, but his main interest was botany and the garden behind his home. He was considered an expert by some of his scientific contemporaries.

The oldest brother, Lewis, is probably the best known of the four. He became Inspector of Customs for Beaumaris and Holyhead *(Caergybi)*. He was commissioned in 1737 to survey some of the Welsh ports for the Admiralty, as before this time they had never been accurately charted. As his work on Anglesey *(Ynys Môn)* was part-time, he spent some of the summer months sailing along the coast in a hired boat, to go out to sea to measure depths, and during the winter he would spend time converting the figures he had collected into detailed charts which covered the coast from Llandudno westwards, around Anglesey *(Ynys Môn)*, Caernarfonshire and south as far as Milford Haven.

Lewis produced an atlas, 'Plans of Harbours, Bars, Bays, and Roads in St George's Channel, including twenty-five detailed plans of Puffin Island and Black Point, Red Wharf Bay, Dulas beach, Cemlyn, Holyhead *(Caergybi)*, Malltraeth, Llanddwyn and Abermenai'. These valuable charts made sailing easier and safer than it had been hitherto.

Lewis Morris was later appointed under-steward for Crown lands in Ceredigion, and left his native Anglesey *(Ynys Môn)*, never to return.

The Morris brothers were an astounding family combination, supporting each other's many interests through their correspondence.

Penrhosllugwy, the area between Dulas and Moelfre, has some of the most important early archaeological sites in Anglesey *(Ynys Môn)*, including a burial chamber with a huge capstone, dating probably from the fourth century. When it was excavated in 1938 fragments of bones of thirty people were found there, along with animal bones, mussel shells and pottery.

Nearby is Din Llugwy, a hut settlement also originating from the fourth century when it was built as a defence against Irish raiders, and remodelled during the Roman occupation of Anglesey *(Ynys Môn)*. This consists of a strongly walled pentagonal enclosure with two circular and several rectangular huts. Judging by its plan and construction, experts believe it could have been the home of an important personage, possibly a chieftain.

Moelfre from the sea is seen as a picturesque village, its old cottages and public house marking the edge of the small, shingle bay, with a prominent lifeboat station.

The Seawatch Centre is the place to visit to be reminded of the area's ever-present association with the sea and all the dangers entailed. Opened in recent years by Ynys Môn County Council, the Centre's displays are grouped around a modern lifeboat, and rightly so as Moelfre has earned a special place in the story of rescue at sea through the exploits of the local crews over the years.

The shipwreck which has been called the most disastrous in Welsh history took place in October 1859 during a hurricane force gale. The weather was unprecedented, taking its toll of life at sea all around the coasts of Britain, with one hundred and thirty-eight ships lost, ninety badly damaged, and around eight hundred lives lost in one night.

North Wales had its share of casualties on that dramatic night. Holyhead *(Caergybi)* breakwater and the Penrhyn pier at Bangor were severely damaged, and no less than forty coastal vessels lay wrecked on the shores of the Menai Strait.

The *Royal Charter* was a large iron steam clipper which had sailed around the world to bring three hundred and ninety passengers home to Liverpool, many of them bringing with them wealth accumulated during the Australian Gold Rush. She was also carrying bullion worth over £300,000. As she entered Liverpool Bay the hurricane struck. The ship was helpless to withstand the mountainous seas and storm force winds, and hit rocks at Porth Helaeth, a cove to the north of Moelfre. Although land was so close, nothing could be done to launch a lifeboat or to save the ship and most of the passengers and crew. After a night of horror the ship broke up, splaying men, women and children into the sea, most of them to be pounded to death on the rocks. As the bodies were washed ashore they were taken to Llanallgo and Llaneugrad churches for identification.

Stephen Roose Hughes, rector of Llanallgo, and his brother Hugh Robert Hughes, curate of Penrhosllugwy, had the harrowing task of helping the bereaved to identify their relatives. Both showed passionate concern. Stephen Roose Hughes replied to more than a thousand letters from victims' families, and the brothers officiated at the funerals of one hundred and forty victims at both churches in a matter of weeks. The bodies of the remaining victims were never recovered. As there was so much valuable cargo, the Crown enlisted the help of twenty local men to collect gold and valuables washed ashore.

A memorial commemorating the event, and those who lost their lives, stands on the cliff north of Moelfre, close to where the ship was wrecked.

Exactly one hundred years later the *Hindlea*, a coaster, was wrecked off the sea-girt rock to the north of Moelfre. She was sailing from Weston Point, Runcorn, to Newport in Gwent and was caught in a gale with waves eight metres high hitting the ship. Moelfre lifeboat went to the rescue, making several attempts, and at one time the lifeboat was blown over the deck of the *Hindlea*. Persistent efforts resulted in the rescue of eight men. Shortly after, the ship was hurled against the rock and broke in two.

It was ironic that the previous day a centenary remembrance service had been held for those lost in the *Royal Charter* wreck.

Moelfre to Llanddona

The eastern side of Anglesey *(Ynys Môn)*, although exposed to winds off the sea, has more trees and wears a more gentle appearance. Today this coast attracts many holiday makers. Caravans stand in tidy parks. The beaches are busy on fine summer days. Water sports are popular. Every small cove has its visitors, and everything in the summer months is geared towards the tourist.

Visitors to Traeth Bychan, who are old enough, will recall the horror when the submarine *Thetis* was grounded here in 1939 after failing to surface during trials in Liverpool Bay. She was a death capsule, containing the ninety-nine bodies of the crew. *Thetis* was later towed away to be re-fitted and renamed *Thunderbolt* to serve in World War II.

Benllech is a sprawl of housing. Its popularity as a holiday resort grew as visitors came to appreciate the fine stretch of sandy beach, many of them enjoying their stay so much that they were determined to end their days here on retirement. And so it has proved. In the Benllech shops you will hear Welsh, Midlands and Lancashire accents.

Every student of Welsh poetry is aware of the association of Goronwy Owen with this area for his story, while true, is legendary. He was trained for the church, but was disillusioned constantly by his clerical and teaching appointments which took him to Shropshire, Liverpool and London and finally America, away from his beloved Wales. Family tragedies added to his depression and his *hiraeth* (longing) for Anglesey *(Ynys Môn)*. This longing was reflected in his poetry. Goronwy died on his own cotton and tobacco plantation in Virginia. George Borrow, on his *Wild Wales* itinerary, made for Llanfair Mathafarn Eithaf expressly to see for himself where the poet had lived as a child.

When the tide is far out, Traeth Coch *(Red Wharf Bay)* is one of the largest tracts of sand off the coast of Anglesey *(Ynys*

Môn). The cluster of buildings along the shoreline are all that is left of a one-time busy little late 18th and 19th century port, with a small ship-building industry. Today the scene is always peaceful even in the height of summer. The little Afon Nodwydd empties itself sinuously through the sand into the bay. Many years ago the tide brought the sea almost up to Pentraeth village – the name, meaning 'head of the strand', confirms this. But now the sea has retreated and the land has reverted to marsh and pasture.

Mynydd Llwydiarth, now almost covered with trees, overlooks Pentraeth. Those trees hide two cairns and the remains of a fort. The seaward-facing side drops steeply down to Traeth Coch where the coastline sweeps around to the little church of Llanddona as the bay opens out to the sea. Although the church, dedicated to Saint Dona, was rebuilt in the 19th century, it has a repaired 15th century doorway. The church stands some way from the village which consists of houses and a chapel scattered at random higher up the hill.

The story of the witches of Llanddona is part of Anglesey *(Ynys Môn)* folklore. It tells how a boat came ashore in the bay without a rudder or oars, full of men and women suffering from exposure, hunger and thirst – it was the custom to put evil doers in an oarless and rudderless boat to drift. They landed at Llanddona, put up shelter and settled. The men were smugglers and the women, it was said, practised witchcraft and begged, and the villagers lived in constant fear of them.

The witches created havoc, harming animals, curdling the milk, and making life impossible for the cottagers. They turned themselves into hares to carry out their mischief unperceived until one of the local men realised what was happening and took out his gun. Into the barrel he put a silver coin instead of shot, as shot could not penetrate a witch's body. When he saw a hare making its way into the byre, he shot it, and ever after the villagers of Llanddona were left in peace.

The beach of Llanddona was the scene of a more realistic

event early in the last century, when it witnessed an early flying experiment. William Ellis Williams, a physicist, had a particular interest in aerodynamic research. While assistant lecturer in physics at the university in Bangor he planned to build his own monoplane, and as he was allowed by a sponsor who was a local landowner to build a hangar in a field at Llanddona, he was able to do so.

When it was completed the light-weight aeroplane, made of ash and bamboo and weighing seventy pounds, was towed on to the flat sandy beach. The test flight took place in September 1913, when Williams achieved a height of seven feet, flying at thirty-seven miles per hour. There is a plaque at the picnic site to commemorate his success.

Llanddona to Penmon

The quarries at Penmon have supplied stone for many important buildings and developments, including the Menai Strait bridges, the lighthouse at South Stack, the harbour at Holyhead *(Caergybi)*, Birmingham Town Hall, and many of the city's fine buildings in Liverpool.

Ynys Seiriol *(Puffin Island)*, the hump of limestone one mile long, is only a short distance from Trwyn Du *(Black Point)* yet access is difficult because of treacherous currents. After visiting Ynys Seiriol during the latter quarter of the 15th century, William Worcester in his *Itinerarium* describes it as being 'separated from the mainland by the distance covered by the flight of two arrows with bow shots' and records seeing its surface 'covered with elder trees'. He also refers to seeing rabbits and adders there.

There was once a great colony of puffins, hence the island's English name, but a count in 1990 revealed fewer than thirty pairs. The same bird count found four hundred pairs of cormorants breeding, which, it was estimated, was over half of the total Welsh cormorant population. There was also a colony of kittiwakes.

When puffins were more abundant they were caught and pickled, and sent in barrels to the cities where they were considered a delicacy. A persistent population of brown rats foraging among the seabird colonies for eggs has accounted for a decrease in some species. Grey seals haul out on to the island and are an attraction to tourists able to take advantage of calm weather to enjoy a boat trip from Beaumaris to see them.

The effect of myxamatosis, which spread throughout Britain in 1954 and 1955, was to change the pattern of plant life on Ynys Seiriol by increasing the numbers of palatable plants growing on the island in the absence of rabbits.

An early religious settlement founded by Saint Seiriol eventually became part of the Augustinian Order. Giraldus

Cambrensis, in his tour of Wales, mentions the fraternity and comments: 'When any discord arises among them by the influence of human passion all their provisions are devoured and destroyed by a species of small mice with which the island abounds. But when the discord ceases they are no longer troubled'.

It is not known how many were in that early monastic fraternity, but burials took place, as human bones have been found. Saint Seiriol's original sanctuary, dated around AD 540, later became the monastery church. Only the tower remains, probably 12th century Norman. Its pyramidical roof is one of three in Anglesey *(Ynys Môn)*, the other two being at Llaneilian and Penmon.

When the semaphore signalling system between Holyhead *(Caergybi)* and Liverpool was introduced, Ynys Seiriol was chosen as one of the station sites. It must have been a lonely existence for the station keeper who would be on constant watch to receive signals from Point Lynas to convey them across Conwy Bay to the Orme at Llandudno.

After the semaphore system went out of use, the signal house was taken over in 1887 by the Liverpool Marine Biology Committee as a laboratory, but they maintained it for only five years before transferring their operations to Port Erin.

Ynys Seiriol has always been regarded as a mystical place. Legends telling of lands beneath the sea are a part of ancient folklore. Whether they are based on fact or fiction is debatable, a question which will never be answered as they are as old as time itself.

Tradition tells of Llys Helyg, the court of a Welsh king in ancient times, which lies submerged at the eastern extremity of Traeth Lafan *(Lafan Sands)*. Helyg ap Glannwg was threatened with vengeance for the crimes his ancestors perpetrated, and was stalked by a wailing voice crying *'Dial a ddaw!'* (vengeance will come!). He held a feast where there was great merrymaking and drinking, to call the bluff of the insistent threat. A great storm arose, with a flood tide which engulfed his hall and he and his family and as many of his servants and guests as could do so had to flee for safety. After the inundation Helyg assumed a religious life as did his twelve children.

The name Traeth Lafan has been connected by Welsh scholar, Ifor Williams to Eflafen, a wharf and a fishing near Aberogwen, but a manuscript of unknown date suggests that Lafan might have come from the word 'aflafan' (unclean), Traeth Lafan meaning 'unpleasant strand'. It goes on to tell the story of the inundation of a large tract of land that stretched from Y Gogarth *(the Orme)* at Llandudno almost to Penmon, of which Traeth Lafan is now a part.

It was so called, claimed the writer, 'because ytt is an unpleasant sight unto the spectators, and a fearfull and dismal objecte unto the eyes of thinhabitantes, bringynge them dayly in mynde how unhappy they weare to loose soe fayre so fruitfull and so fearfill a countrey, beyinge beaten backe with unpleasant overwhelmynge waves to inhabytt and dwell in higher growndds uppon the edges and skyrtes of the hills and mountaynes . . . '

Modern researchers are more prosaic. They put the 'walls' that are revealed by exceptionally low tides down to a natural phenomenon. 'The appearance of walls is illusory', they say. They are an accumulation of stones of glacial origin, pebbles and boulders derived from boulder clay deposited when stone-laden ice melted at the end of the Ice Age.

Saint Seiriol is reputed to have laid a pavement to reach from Ynys Seiriol to another of his cells, at Penmaenmawr across what was then low, marshy ground, before the coast receded to the line it takes today. This is yet another legend, as it is thought the changing coastline happened well before his day. This 'pavement' is nothing more than a submerged reef of carboniferous limestone, say the geologists. So is yet another colourful tradition discredited.

Joseph Sheridan Le Fanu, a great-nephew of Sheridan the

dramatist, wrote two novels, *The Tenants of Mallory* and *Willing to Die*, both inspired by this corner of Anglesey *(Ynys Môn)*. Place-names have been changed, but the author writes so graphically that it is obvious that he has set his stories around Penmon and Beaumaris. He calls Ynys Seiriol Cawdrwydd Island, describing it as 'a phantom island, with now and then a gleam of silver spray from the swell which was unfelt within the estuary, shooting suddenly across its points of shadow'.

Sandbanks at the entrance to the Menai Strait are another hazard to shipping. In 1831 the *Rothsay Castle*, an old, unseaworthy steamer, was bringing passengers from Liverpool to North Wales when she struck the expanse of sand known as Dutchman's Bank in bad weather. The passengers had pleaded with the captain to return to Liverpool, to no avail. The ship sheared off into a channel, then struck again and again and eventually broke up. The captain and the mate were killed as the funnel and the mainmast fell. Beaumaris lifeboat put to sea to the rescue, but could pick up only twenty survivors out of one hundred and fifty passengers and crew. The rest were drowned. One result of this tragedy was the decision to erect the Trwyn Du *(Black Point)* lighthouse on the shore opposite Ynys Seiriol.

The lighthouse was manned at first by two keepers, but they were withdrawn in 1922 when the light was converted to unwatched acetylene operation. Trwyn Du was converted to solar power in 1996 and modernisation included the development of a unique operating mechanism to work the fog bell. The range of light covers twelve sea miles.

A private road belonging to the Baron Hill estate leads from the coastguard lookout at Trwyn Du across heathland to the church, old monastic buildings, the holy well and cell and the dovecote at Penmon.

The Vikings attacked Penmon in the latter years of the 10th century and intermittently afterwards while the Normans were in occupation, and it was not until the Normans abandoned

Ynys Môn and native rulers seized power again that the church at Penmon was built. When Llywelyn Fawr became prince, he granted the monastery at Penmon to the Prior and Canons of Ynys Seiriol and presumably it was then, or soon after, that the monastic buildings were built. By 1414 Penmon was a priory of the order of Saint Augustine. The Prior of Ynys Seiriol removed his seat from the island to Penmon, and that could have been the catalyst for re-building.

Today the ruined buildings cluster around the church, which remains in regular use. It houses treasures, notably some stone carvings in the south transept which include the fertility figure of *Sheila-na-gig* and a bronze plaque of Limoges enamel found near the altar when the chancel was restored in 1855. This is the part of the church now used for services.

The nave has stones displayed which were found in the deer park that encompassed the monastery. In recent years the monks' fish pond has been restored.

Standing apart, yet part of the Penmon complex, is the dovecote, built probably about 1600. It is a square building with a domed roof and an open cupola to allow the birds entry. Inside there are niches for nearly a thousand nests which could be reached by climbing a ladder put up against a central pillar with corbelled steps, twelve feet (3.6m) high.

Penmon sees many visitors on a fine summer day, some paying the toll to use the private road to Trwyn Du, while others are content to saunter around the quiet surroundings of church and monastic buildings and absorb the peaceful atmosphere before returning along the beautiful coastal road towards Beaumaris.

tax-free bikes for work

Cyclescheme

Request your voucher online at:

www.cyclescheme.co.uk/a519e7

Staffordshire
County Council

Staffordshire
County Council

What are the benefits?

◀ **Big savings** on the cost of a new bike and safety equipment
◀ **Pay monthly** and save on VAT, Income Tax and NI
◀ **Get any make & model** from over 1100 local bike shops
◀ **Make your requests** securely online

For more information, visit:

www.cyclescheme.co.uk/a51967

How much can I save?

To find out how much you can save please use the savings calculator at **www.cyclescheme.co.uk/a51967**

What do I do next?

◀ Locate your local partner shops on our website at **www.cyclescheme.co.uk/a51967**

◀ Visit a shop and choose your bike and safety equipment – you will be given a paper quotation

◀ Enter your quotation and digitally sign your Hire Agreement online at **www.cyclescheme.co.uk/a51967**

◀ Staffordshire County Council will check your eligibility and digitally countersign your Hire Agreement

◀ A hire agreement will be sent to your home address, sign and return this document to Cyclescheme Ltd

◀ A secure voucher is sent out to your home address

◀ You redeem the secure voucher in the bike shop upon production of photographic ID

Any questions?

If you have any queries please refer to our website at **www.cyclescheme.co.uk**, contact our helpdesk on 01225 448933 or alternatively please contact:

◀ **Sonia Atkins**, Tel: 01785 276615
Email: sonia.atkins@staffordshire.gov.uk

Penmon to Beaumaris

From where the road from Penmon to Beaumaris skirts the sea, at low tide one can appreciate the huge extent of sandbanks of Traeth Lafan and Dutchman's Bank.

Bedwyr Lewis Jones, whose scholarly researches into the derivation of place-names makes fascinating reading, explains that at one time, following the wars between the Low Countries and England in the 17th century, the epithet 'Dutchman' carried a derogatory connotation. He instances 'Dutch courage' – the false courage of a drunkard. During the days of sailing ships, the sandbank known as Dutchman's Bank was particularly hazardous although it appeared not to be so. The bank is known in Welsh as *Banc yr Hen Wyddeles*.

The sloop-rigged sailing ship *Linnet* was returning from Liverpool to Aberaeron with general cargo in November 1890 when she was hit by a ferocious gale as she attempted to round the Ynys Môn coast. There were three on board, the captain, mate and a twelve-year old boy. The captain decided to anchor near Traeth Coch to ride out the storm, but the anchor broke loose and the ship drifted past Ynys Seiriol and on to Traeth Lafan, where it was stranded. In an attempt to save him, from possible drowning, the boy was lashed to the rigging, but he died. By next morning as the tide receded the *Linnet* was left high and dry on the sand. She was seen by two local men who took to a small boat to take them over the channels to reach the ship. They succeeded in rescuing the captain and the mate, but both died of exposure later.

Where the road leaves the shore at Lleiniog, it climbs through a narrow valley with a marshy bottom. On the hill to the right, hidden by scrub and a copse of trees, are the remains of the Norman castle of Aberlleiniog. The mound is artificial. The first castle, built by Hugh, Earl of Chester in c.1190, would have been of timber, and communication between it and the shore would have been by a sunken way, a good defence. The second building on the site was a stone fort, four sided with round towers at the corners, built during medieval times. During the Civil War this was garrisoned but was surrendered in 1645 and thereafter left to ruin.

Close to the village of Llangoed stands Cornelyn Manor, the one-time home of two exceptional sisters, the Misses Massey. Among their many attributes they were artists who painted some five hundred pictures of Anglesey *(Ynys Môn)* plants and flowers during the 1920s and '30s, one sister specialising in pencil drawings, the other in water colour painting. These are now in safe keeping at Oriel Ynys Môn in Llangefni.

The paintings appear as fresh today as they would have appeared on the day they were painted. The detail is remarkable. One sister also kept two large scrap books, now in the archives of the University of Wales at Bangor. They are full of anecdotes and memories of the Anglesey Hunt fraternity. But their chief attraction is their decoration. Country animals tumble riotously down the margins and along the foot of the pages. The foxes and rabbits are depicted in gold leaf and have riveting glass eyes.

Llanfaes is a small village which existed before nearby Beaumaris had been thought of. Llywelyn ap Iorwerth founded a monastery of Franciscan friars here and this is where he buried his wife, Siwan (Joan) in 1237. The friary was erected over her grave. But it had a chequered existence. When Henry IV led an army to Anglesey *(Ynys Môn)* against Owain Glyndŵr the friars were supportive of the Welshmen, and Henry partially destroyed the friary and the monks left. His successor, Henry V, granted a new charter to Llanfaes so the monastery was re-built, but it fell once more in 1536 at the Dissolution. Siwan's coffin was found, and it now stands in the porch of Beaumaris parish church.

Later, a house was built on the monastery site, called 'Fryars'. In 1940 it was taken over by what is now the Lairds Group and a factory erected in the grounds for the manufacture of parts for Catalina flying boats and equipment for the Ministry of Defence during the Second World War. Workmen building a slipway across the road to Penmon uncovered human bones, believed to be the remains of some of the occupants of the old friary.

Trees crown the higher land behind the Strait's shoreline at Llanfaes, and the large mansion of Baron Hill, once the seat of the Bulkeley family for centuries, lies hidden. It is a shadow of its former glory, a great house allowed to fall into ruin. But the name of Bulkeley is seen everywhere in Beaumaris, reminding one of the influence this important family had on Anglesey *(Ynys Môn)* life. After the death of one member of the family in the 1860s the large obelisk standing on the crest of the hill was put up in his memory.

Edward I, building his fortifications to ring the coast of Wales, decided his final castle should be on land close to Llanfaes. Building began in 1295, after the population of Llanfaes had been moved over to Rhosyr on the west coast and the new town called Niwbwrch *(Newborough)*.

Beaumaris

The shipping channel called Fryar's Road skirts the Anglesey *(Ynys Môn)* shore and gives the sailor an overall view of the attractive town of Beaumaris. Not so many years ago, the town was only half its present size. Since, housing development at Cae Mair has pushed the boundary out in the direction of Porthaethwy. Property prices here reflect the desirability of their outstanding position and the breathtaking view most of them command across the town to the water, the mountains and over Conwy Bay to Llandudno.

From the sea, Beaumaris appears to sit comfortably against a background of rising fields and woods. The front is dominated by the elegant hotel and terrace of tall Victorian houses which take away one's attention from the nearby castle.

Beaumaris castle is the most symmetrical, concentrically-planned castle in Britain. It was built with a labour force of four hundred masons, two thousand labourers, thirty smiths and carpenters. By 1298, three years after work began, it could have been defended. Then, for a quarter of a century after, building continued only slowly and parts of the original plan were never carried out.

The castle saw some action at the time of the Glyndŵr rising in the 15th century, and was put in a state of defence during the Civil War but saw no actual fighting. From then on it deteriorated. Lead and timber were filched, and some of the stones put to use elsewhere in the town. Since 1925 it has been partially restored under the watchful eyes of the Ministry of Public Buildings and Works and CADW.

Edward I gave the name Beaumaris (beautiful marsh) to this part of Llanfaes. A new town grew outside its walls and its position, near the entrance to the Menai Strait, contributed to its success as a port in later years, when many vessels were registered here.

Beaumaris received its charter from Edward in 1296.

Trading gathered impetus over the years, and by 1600 the town was an important postal town, necessary in the Crown service of seeing that mail passed safely on its way to Holyhead (*Caergybi*) and so to Ireland, or south to England. It also had a customs office.

Inns were built as early as the late 16th or early 17th centuries – the George and Dragon and the Bulls Head are early examples, with the Liverpool Arms following· in 1700 – all to meet demand from travellers who made the difficult crossing from the mainland over Traeth Lafan before continuing on the last lap of their journey to Holyhead (*Caergybi*).

As the town prospered, amenities were needed. David Hughes, an Anglesey (*Ynys Môn*) man who was appointed steward to the manor of Woodrising in Norfolk, left money in his will to found a Grammar School in Beaumaris in 1602. The building, much altered, still stands by the side of the castle moat. It housed the Grammar School up to the introduction of comprehensive education in Anglesey (*Ynys Môn*) in 1962, when pupils were transferred to a purpose-built new school in Porthaethwy, which now carries his name. The old school in Beaumaris is now a community centre.

The administration of law and order centred on Beaumaris for several centuries. The 1614 courthouse, where Assizes were held as late as 1971, is now a tourist attraction as little has been done to alter it internally since it was so used.

The tower of the parish church can be seen over the roof tops from the sea. There has been a church on the site since the 14th century, but the chancel was rebuilt in 1500. Carved misericords, fine stained glass, a venerable organ and interesting memorials all serve to make the parish church of Saint Mary and Saint Nicholas a building of note.

Not all the features of Beaumaris can be appreciated from the sea, however. One needs to wander down its narrow streets to find the gaol in Steeple Lane. Built in 1829 to a design by Joseph Hansom of Hansom cab fame, the gaol is now a museum. It was once a model prison. Records give details of the inmates, the crimes they perpetrated and the punishment meted out to them. The prison's most famous inmate was Richard Rowlands, the last prisoner to be hanged. Newspaper reports of 1862 describe the event, attended by crowds who had come from all over the island to witness the execution. His last act, the story goes, was to curse the church clock as he stepped out to the scaffold. Researches have since given strong credence to the belief that Richard Rowlands was, in fact, not guilty – his wife testified to this on her death bed. Could this be the reason that the hands on the face of the church clock opposite the gaol have been erratic ever since? Tradition would have it so.

The first gaol was in the castle. The purpose-built gaol in Steeple Lane was closed in 1878 and afterwards used as a lock-up and police station, and re-opened as a museum in 1975.

As time passed, and travel was made easier, there was an influx of holiday visitors to the island. Beaumaris was a major attraction. The views across to the mountains, the pier, and the wide green on the sea front were unsurpassed and the Victorians arrived in the steamers from Liverpool which called at the pier on their way to Porthaethwy.

Sailing regattas attracted the more active, and yachtsmen were catered for at the newly-opened Royal Anglesey Yacht Club, where they still congregate. Although the existing inns and boarding houses offered accommodation, more modern and up-market facilities were needed and so the Bulkeley Arms Hotel was built in a commanding position near to the pier. Joseph Hansom, its architect, also designed the Victoria Terrace, since converted into apartments, which raised the status of the town well beyond what any other town in Anglesey *(Ynys Môn)* could offer. The image of a fashionable Victorian watering place had come to stay.

When the Menai suspension bridge was opened, the Bulkeley family at Baron Hill found the winding road through Llandegfan to Menai Bridge *(Porthaethwy)* inconvenient, and built the picturesque road that hugs the coast, giving tantalising glimpses through the trees of the mainland opposite. Where that road begins at the western end of Beaumaris is a marina and chandler's depot marking Gallows Point.

From here, Telford's suspension bridge comes into view, and it is only a short sail to St George's Pier at Menai Bridge *(Porthaethwy)* where the cruise around Anglesey *(Ynys Môn)* began.

Further Reading

Aled Eames, *Ships and Seamen of Anglesey*.

Transactions of the Anglesey Antiquarian Society and Field Club – various.

E.A Williams, *The Day Before Yesterday* (trans. G. Wynne Griffith).

Francis Henry Glazebrook, *Anglesey and the North Wales Coast*.

The National Trust, *The Hidden World of the Menai*.

Tom Bennett, *Shipwrecks around Wales*, vol. 2.

John L. Williams, *Llanfairpwllgwyngyll, hen enwau a lluniau'r lle*.

William Condry, *Exploring Wales*.

Royal Commission, Anglesey: Survey and Inventory by the Royal Commission on Ancient and Historical Monuments in Wales and Monmouthshire.

Jeffrey Morgan Lewis, *Llanedwen Church on the Isle of Anglesey*.

David Senogles, *A History of the Parish of Llandysilio*.

T.T.M. Hale, *Rhosneigr Then and Now*.

Môn, Mam Cymru, the Anglesey Guide.

W. Eifion Jones (ed.), *A New Natural History of Anglesey*.

Ordnance Survey, Jarrold, *Snowdonia, Anglesey and the Lleyn Peninsula*.

Edwin Roland Owens, *Mynydd Twr* (Holyhead Mountain).

William Hywel, *The Modest Millionaire*.

Gwilym Trefor Jones and Tomos Roberts, *Enwau Lleoedd Môn*.

The essential guide to Cemaes, Anglesey.

John S. Rees, *History of the Liverpool Pilotage Service*.

F.J. North, *Sunken cities: some legends of the coast and lakes of Wales*.